Caring for Creation:
Toward an Ethic of Responsibility

Anne Rowthorn

MOREHOUSE PUBLISHING
WILTON, CONNECTICUT

Morehouse Publishing
78 Danbury Road
Wilton, Connecticut 06897

Library of Congress Cataloging-in-Publication Data
Rowthorn, Anne W.
Caring for creation: toward an ethic of responsibility/Anne Rowthorn.
p.   cm.
Bibliography: p.
Includes index.
ISBN 0-8192-1506-6
1. Ecology, Human—Religious aspects—Christianity. 2. Ecology, Human—
Moral and ethical aspects. 3. Creation. 4. Nature—Religious aspects—
Christianity. 5. Nature—Moral and ethical aspects. I. Title.
BT695.5.R68   1989
241'.691—dc20   89-32725
                                                        CIP

Cover photography by R. Krubner/H. Armstrong Roberts, Inc.
Cover design by Carole Masonberg

Printed in the United States of America
by
BSC LITHO
Harrisburg, PA

Epigraphs

For those who have seen the earth from space . . . the experience most certainly changes your perspective. The things we share in our world are far more valuable than those which divide us.

——Donald Williams
U.S.A.[1]

The first day or so we all pointed to our countries. The third or fourth day we were pointing to our continents. By the fifth day we were aware of only one Earth.

——Sultan Bin Salman al-Saud
Saudi Arabia[2]

Before I flew I was already aware of how small and vulnerable our planet is; but only when I saw it from space, in all its ineffable beauty and fragility, did I realize that humankind's most urgent task is to cherish and preserve it for future generations.

——Sigmund Jahn
German Democratic Republic[3]

We were flying over America and suddenly I saw snow, the first snow we ever saw from orbit . . . and then it struck me that we are all children of the Earth. It does not matter what country you look at. We are all Earth's children, and we should treat her as our mother.

——Aleksandr Aleksandrov
U.S.S.R.[4]

Dedication

*To
Virginia,
Christian,
and
Perry
with love*

Contents

The Deadly Duel

Acknowledgments

No book is written without the generous sharing of ideas, encouragement, and resources on the part of many. In this regard I am grateful to Joe Coelho, John Docker, Prudence Randall, Russell Schulz-Widmar, Bill Lupher, Philip Turner, and Steve Charleston. They each sent or lent me pertinent articles and books or otherwise brought them to my attention. Special thanks are owed to my mother, Elisabeth S. Bundy, for her continuing interest in this project and because she introduced me to Granny Dodge (who appears in Chapter 1). I am grateful to my fellow members of Witness for Disarmament, particularly Arthur Laffin, editor (with Anne Montgomery) of *Swords Into Plowshares: Nonviolent Direct Action For Disarmament*, as well as Michael Drummy, Bob Sireno, Suzanne Abrams, and other members. They have gently taught me what it means to back up belief in the goodness of God's Creation with the loving action of one's life, even when such action may lead to the courtroom and the jail cell. In the preparations of this book, I have benefited greatly from the many constructive suggestions and help of my editors at Morehouse Publishing: E. Allen Kelley and Deborah Grahame-Smith, as well as from Carole Masonberg, the designer and production manager. I am particularly grateful for the presence in my life of my dear husband, Jeffery. He has been a ready partner in the discussion of all the issues covered in this book, and, as always, his insights and questions stimulated and expanded my imagination. This book is a better book because of his help.

For this project, I owe my greatest debt to our three children. Like their father, they were lusty partners in the exchange of ideas and sources. The glow of their youthful idealism has not yet grown dull (and I hope it never will). They think in fresh ways and render the texture of life in vivid colors with broad brush strokes. Also they have helped immeasurably in practical ways. Christian added to may sources on Native American culture, ecology, and comparative religion; Perry assisted with antinuclear and peace materials; and because of Virginia, a Peace Corps volunteer in the Marshall Islands, I spent a preparatory six months studying the cultural and political issues of the Pacific Islands and spent several weeks of total immersion with her and her Marshallese family on Mili Island in Mili Atoll.

I am indebted to my children for who they are and for all that they have taught me. I am moved by their laughter and humor, by their passion for life, and by their developing sense of social responsibility. These children—and all children everywhere—are God's hope, and, indeed, they are the hope of the world. Therefore this book is dedicated to them.

Introduction

Humankind is at the crossroads. We live at the unique time in the history of the world when our species—the human species—has the capacity to destroy every bit of created life: all animal life, all human life, all plant life, all oceans and rivers—everything we know, everything we love and hold dear; our friends and families; our reason, our imaginations, our passions, our pleasures, ourselves; everything. Everything we are and every aspect of God's Creation is in peril.

Humankind is at the crossroads, at the junction between life and death, future and the abyss, in large measure because the church is at the crossroads. The church's inability to affirm the world as God's own Creation, to affirm it generously and wholeheartedly, has brought us to this point. Christians' lack of appreciation for the connectedness of all of life, both natural and animal, as well as our lack of recognition of our dependence upon the natural world, has brought us to this point. The church's dualistic approach to the world that says some of life is sacred, the rest secular, has brought us to this point. If we genuinely looked with God's eyes at all that God created and said with our Creator, "Behold it is very good" (Gen. 1:31, adapted), Christians would not tolerate the rape of the land by acid rain, by pesticides; we would not tolerate the destruction of precious topsoil from midwestern farmlands, nor the poisoning of our rivers and oceans, nor the pollution of the air we breathe. Bikini Island, Three Mile Island, and Chernobyl would be mere locations, not symbols of nuclear death traps; and none of us would abide the nightmare knowledge of fifty thousand nuclear weapons stashed away in arsenals around the world, fearful of the half hour it would take to ignite them and destroy everything that is or might have been.

By virtue of the fact that our gracious God called the world into being and loves it, Christians are obliged to love it and to care for it. Because of God's movement in Creation, because of God's tender care for all created life, the well-being of the world and all its people is, or ought to be, the church's first consideration.

Christians have, by and large, acted as if the holy, the sacred, were to be found within the structures of the church rather than in the world. A high value has been placed on the retreat, the monastic experience, the encounter with God within formal religious institutions. And because of the loss of the cosmic view of God's Creation, it is understandable that Christian service within religious institutions has historically come to be regarded as being more important than Christian service in the world. Christian service has become equated with service to God and to God's people within the religious community.

The church's urgent need to embrace an ethic of Creation has been affirmed by John Baker, Anglican Bishop of Salisbury in England. In a paper entitled "Making Christianity More Christian," Baker stated that

> the job [of Christians] is to be friends of Jesus in the world. They are those who . . . know that God loves the world, and live their lives as members of the world. They have only one agenda item: so to live in every place that the world in that place becomes truly the family and realm of God.[1]

This book was begun well before the terrible summer of 1988, and as the summer progressed I realized even more how very timely the book's theme is. As I was pushing to finish the final chapters, the American people were tired from choking on the weeks of extreme heat and pollution. There were nightly news reports of drought-stricken farmlands and distressed farmers whose crops had been ruined. Beaches were clogged with waste and contamination. Yellowstone National Park was on fire and out of control with more and more acres being burned every day. During the summer the hazards of our national nuclear weapons plants began to come into public awareness, and there were dire warnings about what will happen if the greenhouse effect goes unchecked. Nightly newscasts were like reruns of the environmental issues I'd spent each day writing about.

Urgently needed is an ethic of responsibility that will expand the vision of all Christians to care for and protect and love all of God's Creation, an ethic that will nurture the expression of faith in action in society, an ethic that calls for deep respect for every aspect of God's world, both natural and human. The economist E.F. Schumacher said,

> At present there can be little doubt that the whole of mankind is in mortal danger, not because we are short of scientific and technological know-how, but because we tend to use it destructively. . . .[2]

Schumacher's solution is a profound reorientation of science, technology, and macroeconomics. To make that happen, nothing short of a religious reconversion to the world will be required.

Nothing short of a total turnaround will empower all of God's people to go through the crossroads into the world's future.

The following is both a warning and a personal note. First the warning: This book is unashamedly written from a personal perspective. What does the declining quality of daily life and of the environment mean to me and to my household? How are my loved ones and I personally affected? What changes in our world and in our society have I noticed in my lifetime? How are our national habits of materialism, consumerism, and consumption affecting our children? What kind of world am I—and my peers—passing on to my own children and all children everywhere?

As I have attempted to address these questions I have taken as a starting point my most immediate surroundings, followed by observations I have made in my travels. I have taken this approach not because my story is particularly noteworthy or unique. Far from it. Rather it is for three reasons. The first is because of the very *ordinariness* of my situation. Let me explain. Since our "civilized" world is affecting me in such profound ways, it therefore stands to reason that it is also affecting you. Thus I would like you to add *your own experience* to the thread of my narrative so that this becomes our shared story and our journey together. And then together we will try to extend our joint experience in an effort to imagine how other world citizens—far less privileged and fortunate than ourselves —are affected. Second, I have taken this approach as a means of making the conditions of our environment and world accessible to me and, by extension, to you also. If I can develop the conscious eye and an understanding heart to begin to understand the complex issues of the environment close at hand, perhaps I can extrapolate and extend that understanding so as to develop a worldview. And third, presenting the issues in a personal way, I hope, will more immediately result in action to reform and renew Creation, for in the long run it does not matter to me whether you read this book, but *it does matter greatly* that all of us act in Creation.

I would, therefore, like to have this book regarded as an extended conversation between reader and author, a conversation that—if you like—is a prelude and a preparation for action.

Now the warning: There will be several places in this book where you may want to turn off, especially chapter 2. Don't! As the author, I realize that I have taken a certain risk in writing chapter 2 because the issues it deals with are upsetting. Furthermore, it seems that we are being bombarded by them from every quarter. Thus, the reader's natural inclination may be to say, "I've had enough," and quit. Reader, I want you to know that I understand that feeling, yet I also want you to know that I felt a responsibility to present, in as concise a way as possible, the facts and figures of our civilization, even at the risk of possibly losing a few readers. So this much I will suggest. Read and absorb what you can of chapter 2. If it gets to you, turn to chapter 7 in which concrete solutions are suggested or perhaps chapter 6 about the refreshing wisdom of native cultures. And then go back to chapter 2.

I hope this book will be seen as testimony that there is indeed light at the end of the tunnel and there is great hope if we will but open our eyes and see it and if we will take the necessary action.

It is ironic that the advanced technology of the developed nations, which has brought us to the brink of disaster, has *also* placed a few world citizens in the unique position to comprehend the acute urgency of acting without delay in order to restore and preserve our fragile planet. James Irwin, a U.S. astronaut, seeing the earth from the perspective of space, observed that this "beautiful, warm, living object looked so fragile, so delicate, that if you touched it with a finger it would crumble and fall apart. Seeing this has changed a man, has to make a man appreciate the creation of God and the love of God."[3] And from the same perspective, Yuri Artyukhin, a Soviet cosmonaut, said, "It isn't important in which sea or lake you observe a slick of pollution, or in the forests of which country a fire breaks out, or on which continent a hurricane arises. *You are standing guard over the whole of our Earth.*"[4]

As with the astronauts and cosmonauts, so with us. We, too, stand as guards over the whole of our earth, and the critical question for us is, What kind of guards will we be? Will we care for Creation with responsibility and with love?

"Today I set before you life and death, blessing and curse. Therefore choose life, that you and your descendants may live." (Deut. 30:19).

How shall we love thee, holy hidden Being, if we love not the world which thou hast made?

——Laurence Houseman

1. Granny Dodge's World

When I first met Granny Dodge, I was already the mother of three children—so I could hardly have been described as merely an impressionable young innocent. Impressionable perhaps, but neither young nor innocent. And had it not been that my mother was the new wife of Granny Dodge's son, Ernest, we would surely never have met.

Granny Dodge is an old Maine woman who has lived all her life on the small islands off the Maine coast and in the tiny communities near Ellsworth. She has rarely left her locale. When she did go once to visit a son in Arizona, her physical reaction to the change was so intense that the intended two-week visit lasted a mere two days. She has taken several trips to Boston, but they have been short (and better) because, as she says, "I can go by car."

Granny lives today much as she has for the last seventy-five years, on the edge of the Union River Bay, in an area known as Bayside. Until several years ago (when she moved across the street to live with her daughter), Granny presided over the family affairs in a small, red farmhouse with neat, white trim, caring for her husband, George, and her three children. From the living room (which was also the dining room, sewing room, recreation room, game room, etc.) Granny could look out to the barn and beyond to the spacious field filled with apple trees. From the tiny parlor—rarely used except for "guests," that is, anyone who was not really

1

a friend or family member, like "summer people"—was an excellent view of the rushing waters of the Union River with the lush Blue Hills beyond. A tar road lay between the house and shore, but it was quiet, mainly used by those who also lived at Bayside.

The living room was indeed the living room. It was the center of the house where the family lived and carried on all of its indoor activities. An enormous fireplace with built-in ovens occupied one whole wall. There was a table to the side, which was variously a desk where the children struggled with their homework, the office where accounts were added up and bills paid, the kitchen table where meals were prepared, and the dining table where they were eaten. In front of the window was a comfortable "settee," as Granny called it, covered with a bright array of crocheted afgans, colorful patchwork quilts, and comfortable pillows. It was the only soft piece of furniture in the room, and those who arrived first scrambled for places on it. Latecomers (if they were children, that is, adults always had a guaranteed place on the settee if they wanted it) sat on the hardwood, straight-back chairs or stretched out on the floor in front of the fireplace on Granny's braided rug (or, to be more accurate, on the *pile* of braided rugs, for the floor was insulated with several layers of them—the newest one placed on top of the heap).

The only accommodations to "progress" in the house were electricity, installed about twenty-five years ago, and a kitchen and bathroom built more recently off the side of the living room. Until then, Granny cooked all the meals at the fireplace. Electricity and a kitchen made it possible for her to have an electric stove and, in the living room, a huge refrigerator and a television—back then invariably turned on to the "Lawrence Welk Show," her favorite, or Liberace, a close second.

Granny went "up to the National"—the First National Supermarket —once every two weeks if she could get a ride. Other than that, she carried on the daily affairs of her life at Bayside just as she always had. She planted and tended the garden, canned and "laid by" vegetables for the winter. She gathered mussels, crabs, wild blueberries, and edible ferns from the shore. She cleaned and dried fish caught out of the bay.

One of her pastimes was the making of extrordinarily beautiful hooked rugs. She made them out of grain sacks and cotton remnants from the textile mill a few miles away in Bangor. They were tapestries of Granny's daily life. The scenes depicted on the rugs were taken from the natural portraits that surrounded her life: the barn and house, the fishing boat. There were the odd yachts of the summer people that were sometimes anchored in the bay, deer and seagulls, apple trees and flowers. There were designs of the granite boulders and the pine trees that hugged the shore across the street. These rugs Granny sold to the summer people. For her own house she made braided rugs that were more ordinary and utilitarian, also bigger. They "cover better," Granny told me.

George, Granny's husband who had died several years before I met the family, passed his time by carving wooden objects for both function and amusement: lobster buoys, axe handles, toys for the children, and even simple musical instruments. One of the toys that survived into the present was "Dancin' Dan," a floppy stick-doll held together by brass pins—a figure that, according to Granny, looked "just like the dancin' man on the Lawrence Welk Show." And when Dancin' Dan was positioned on a flexible board and rhymically tapped, he did his own tap dance.

Granny was a living reservoir of poems, jingles, and nonsense rhymes that dropped from her lips with the greatest of ease and to the delight of the children. The following is a favorite:

H—U—Uckle; B—U—Uckle; H—U—Uckle—I;
B—U—Uckle; C—U—Uckle; Huckleberry pie.

Try it. It's catchy. And Granny had stories with which she entertained several generations of children and their parents. It is her story-telling that ushered her into my life, setting her apart from other old women of character I have known. Through her stories, her remarkable variety of true tales, I was introduced to a worldview radically different than mine: more wholesome, more enriching, one could even say more primordial. I had experienced something of her outlook many years previously among Native Americans with whom I had once spent a summer in a small community on a South Dakota Indian reservation, but Granny is far closer to home. None of this is to say that Granny's world was easy or devoid of hardship. Nor would I call Granny and those of her world either simple or primitive, although, of course, simplicity was one of the hallmarks of Granny's life. It was a world where people lived lives of unity and accommodation to the environment, respectful of its beauty and appreciative of its powers as well as of its dangers.

The time when Granny told me about her experiences with the deer that pranced through her field, I knew instinctively that I was in the presence of someone from a more gracious age. As an old lady just shy of one hundred, Granny used to tell me of the long hours she spent sitting on the living room settee gazing out of the window into the field and even listening to the field. In the fall she would observe the deer nibbling the fallen apples. Granny also gathered the windfalls. The good ones she used for pies and for canning. The less than perfect ones she kept in a large bucket for the wintertime when snow would cover the landscape. Because she felt the deer to be her friends, she reasoned that they would miss the apples of autumn. So when in the depths of winter they came close to her house, Granny would quietly steal from her door and scatter a handful on the ground. The deer must have known Granny to be friendly, for they would often stand stationary in their tracks when she went out, as if unafraid. And, at times, they went about their business of enjoying the treat, hardly aware of Granny's presence at all. When asked why she fed the deer, she couldn't answer except to say that she liked to see them happy. Granny felt a keen bond with the animals. She knew the regulars and those who only stopped by occasionally. When a particular deer hadn't been seen for several weeks, she missed it and rejoiced upon its return.

Ernest Dodge, Granny Dodge's son who inherited his mother's lyrical nature, recorded the richness of her world (and his) in his last book. He called the book *Morning Was Starlight: My Maine Boyhood* because the sky was lit by stars on the winter mornings when he set out from home to walk the six miles to school in Ellsworth. The natural world—seasons, the weather, animals, plants, the tides—became ingrained in the texture of Ernest's life, just as it was in his mother's. In talking about those starlight mornings and about the Bayside Road where he lived, Ernest said,

> The familiarity of its hills and slight bends, the changes of its surface, especially for the six miles from the old farm to downtown Ellsworth, are one of the inescapable ingredients of my life. Its early influence became ingrained in my marrow. For three solid years in every kind of weather, I walked close to twelve miles a day to high school and back. There is no condition under which I have not experienced the Bayside Road's idiosyncrasies—every weather condition, temperatures from high nineties to forty below zero, the flowers that bloomed along the wayside, and the not inconsiderable bird and animal life, the varieties of trees and shrubs, and, above all, the changes in all things constantly brought about by the seasons.[1]

And he went on to say that "a good road leads a man easily and quickly from his home to the outer horizon and beyond."[2] The road did indeed lead Ernest to the outer horizon, for he became a worldwide traveler, a museum director, and an ethnologist of international reputation. The South Pacific islands and the expeditions of Captain Cook became his specialties, and although he authored a number of volumes related to those activities, his favorite book was his last. It is eloquent testimony to a certain attitude and a way of seeing the world.

It was a world of great natural plenty and extravagant beauty but little materially. When the first of the Dodge children was born,

George ended his tenure on an outer island where he had been a lighthouse keeper and never again had what one would consider a real job. There were the family garden, apples, and wild fruit. There were the edible gifts of the shore. Fuel was never a problem, and the house was always warm in winter, for the Dodges' woods were thick with timber.

George knew which varieties of fish were running and where they could best be caught. He kept the family well supplied, and the extra he sold to the townspeople up in Ellsworth. He also knew the best spots for trapping lobsters. The sale of these gifts from the sea provided such cash as the family needed and augmented the income from the sale of Granny's hooked rugs.

> [Lumbering], coasting, fishing, lobstering, and farming all thrived. . . . Everyone worked at all of them at one time of year or another. There was little money and nearly everything was grown or raised.[3]

For their well-being, country people of Granny Dodge's day had to be wise. They needed to know the meaning of the small, black thunderheads appearing in the northwestern sky. Rainbows, a ring around the moon, sun dogs in the sky, the ways the leaves turn and the wind changes direction, the rain song of the robin, the varieties of Maine fog—all these bore intimately on the welfare, and sometimes even the survival, of country folk.

> The chorus of spring peepers, the flash of fire flies in June, the long lines of geese going north and south, the flight of swallows, the run of alewives in the brooks, the shedding of the stag's antlers, all these things take on an added meaning, for they are one with the doings of man and they tell him something about the mere fact of their occurrence. Will the potato seeds rot in the ground? Will the hay in the meadows be lush? Will the cranberries be wormy? Are the combs of the fowl likely to freeze? These things are important, life becomes more bountiful with their understanding.[4]

Granny Dodge could easily be dismissed as being quaint, charming, surely an interesting individual, but not someone to be taken too seriously, for she is but a relic of a bygone age. And my fascination with her and with her worldview could be equally dismissed as romantic and unrealistic.

But I think Granny and all the Granny Dodges of this world (country people like Granny as well as such indigenous people as Eskimo, Native Americans, the Indians of Central and South America) are in touch with a certain reality of being that, for the health and continuation of Creation, those of the "developed world" could be greatly enriched by tapping into and in some measure actually reappropriating. The Granny Dodges have a profound lesson to teach, if we will but listen.

If there is one commonality among indigenous cultures, whether they be Eskimo, Native American, Kalahara Desert people, Pacific Islanders, Manchuria natives, Quechua Indians of South America, and the like, it is this: the sharing of a primordial affinity with the land. It is a relationship of innate respect for other living creatures, a relationship in which animals are regarded as beings, not things. It is an innate sense of awareness of the weather, of seasons and subtle climactic changes. It is, as Barry Lopez has termed it, a "native eye."[5]

Walking Buffalo, a Stony Indian of Canada, was adopted as a child by white missionaries and educated in their schools. He never lost his native eye, and years later he attempted to describe just what this native sense is:

> We saw the Great Spirit's work in almost everything: sun, moon, trees and mountains. Sometimes we approach him through these things. Was that so bad? I think we have true belief in the supreme being, a stronger faith than that of most whites who have called us pagans. . . . Indians living close to nature and nature's rules are not living in darkness.
>
> Did you know that trees talk? Well, they do. They talk to each other, and they talk to you if you listen. [White people] never learned to listen to the Indians so I don't suppose they'll listen to other voices in nature. But I have learned alot from trees: sometimes about animals, sometimes about the Great Spirit.[6]

Detractors will be quick to point out that for all the Granny Dodges and indigenous people who live out a certain relationship with the land there can be cited just as many other examples of indigenous people who have not respected the environment. For all we know, cave dwellers moved from cave to cave, befouling each before going on the next and so on. As Rene Dubos has pointed out, Stone Age people killed far more game than they could eat; they were responsible for the extinction of several large animal species at the end of the Pleistocene period; and the Maoris brought about the extinction of the eagle, the rail, the goose, the swan, and the moa in New Zealand.[7]

And it is also true that "civilized people" have had a continuing on-again, off-again love affair with nature and the natural world. There were the hermits and desert fathers of the early Christian era who left their urban communities for solace in the wilderness. The Alps became the lungs for rich, urban sophisticates who wished to "get away from it all." William Wordsworth thrived in the gentle beauty of the English Lake District, and the memory of that great American naturalist, John Muir, continues to cast a long shadow over our own western wilderness. Yellowstone and Yosemite parks were acquired just before the turn of the century by the government so that American and foreign visitors could enjoy them as locations of exceptional beauty where rare species of wild animals could be observed and appreciated in their natural habitat. These parks became cornerstones of the national park system, which has grown to include several dozen parks. And finally, parks of all sizes and shapes continue to be added to the cityscapes of the world.

Nonetheless, "civilized people," constructive as their motives may have been, have not, generally speaking, had the same symbiotic relationship with the land as Granny Dodge has. Their aim was *to use* the natural world to their own ends (for recreation, refreshment, relaxation, etc.—not bad aims in themselves) rather than *to appreciate it for itself and for its own utility* and to blend in with its rhythm. They have failed to acknowledge and respect their dependence upon it.

Citing just one indigenous culture, the Eskimo, which is typical of many, one notes a different attitude than ours:

> A fundamental difference between our culture and Eskimo culture is we have irrevocably separated ourselves from the world that animals occupy. We have turned all animals and elements of the natural world into objects. We manipulate them to serve the complicated ends of our destiny. Eskimos do not grasp this separation easily. . . . For them to make this separation is analogous to cutting oneself off from light or water. . . .
>
> [And] because we have objectified animals, we are able to treat them impersonally. . . . For Eskimos, most relationships with animals are local and personal, [they are] part of one's community, and one has relationship with them.[8]

> The aspiration of aboriginal people throughout the world has been to achieve a congruent relationship with the land, to fit well in it.[9]

Deep within the psyche of "civilized people" there lies a thread—however hidden and tenuous—linking us to our primordial past; it is a link connecting us to a more natural, a more pristine state of awareness. If it were not so, how would one explain such popular activities as camping? Why is it that we are drawn to leave comfortable homes to spend days at a time living under canvas or nylon, cooking simply under the shadow of pine, wiling away whole evenings at a time doing nothing more productive than tending campfires and gazing into them? Or, without leaving home, why are we drawn to suppers cooked in the backyard over clumsy charcoal grills? The same hotdog that emerges from the backyard barbecue pit as black and burned as the charcoal that cooked it would be rejected outright were it to come from the electric stove in the kitchen a few feet away.

Or what is it that entices people on wilderness adventures, big game African photo safaris, rafting expeditions down the Colorado River, and cross-country skiing through Yellowstone Park in the depths of winter? One of my sons camped for two weeks by himself in Yellowstone's backcountry, way off beaten trails, carrying only such supplies as he needed on his back. He did the same in the Arizona desert. When I asked him why, this normally articulate young man was at a loss to answer. I sensed that he was following that inner thread that connects him to his (and our) primordial past.

The Guayaquil Airport in Ecuador is a gathering place for a motley array of people. There are Dallas bankers and Fort Worth cattle barons, California film producers, best-selling authors, successful building contractors from Phoenix, Yale professors, Cleveland realtors, New York City stockbrokers. They are all well heeled or they wouldn't be there, and they are all assembled for one purpose: to board a plane for the Galapagos Islands, some 600 miles off the coast in the nowhere territory of the mid-Pacific. Why would they travel so far and at such great cost to visit thirteen desolate lava piles with little useful vegetation? Of one of the islands, Charles Darwin said, "The whole of this has [a] sterile, dry appearance . . . I think it would be difficult to find in the intertropical latitudes a piece of land 75 miles long, so entirely useless."[10] What is the appeal of such "entirely useless" land? Barrenness notwithstanding, the Galapagos Islands were so special that they inspired Darwin in a course of events that was to become his lifework—namely, the development of his theory of evolution published a quarter of a century after his short visit to the Galapagos.

There is a courtyard in Christ's College, Cambridge, with immaculately tended gardens and flower beds. Above it is the window of the room where Charles Darwin lived when he was a student there. Sitting in that stately, staid, ever-so-civilized English garden courtyard, as I have done on occasion, sets one to wondering what it was that impelled the innocent twenty-two-year-old Darwin—a wealthy landlubber who, by his own admission, had no tolerance for seasickness—to set out on a five-year world voyage aboard the uncomfortable *Beagle*, spending weeks at a time at sea but actually only slightly more than month in the Galapagos.

And what is it about the Galapagos Islands that is so special that such diverse writers as Kurt Vonnegut, Jr., on the one hand, and Annie Dillard, on the other, would be intrigued enough to write about them? Vonnegut's novel, set in a future time, is simply called *Galapagos*, for there time, and even centuries, lacks meaning. One is transported back in time, so why not also eons into the future? Both authors suggest that being in the Galapagos is like being in a latter-day Garden of Eden before the Fall.

I think that the attraction of the Galapagos Islands is that they represent a primeval era, a time before time, as it were. It is as if the islands and empires of all recorded history had risen and fallen, leaving the Galapagos entirely untouched, unscathed, and forgotten. For there is something fundamentally unique about these lava piles. Animal species, found nowhere else on the face of the earth, are there in great profusion: a large variety of unusual birds; also huge tortoises—unique both by their size and age—and giant iguanas. Remarkably, some of these animals are tame. They appear to have missed a connection. Somewhere in their genetic makeup they seem to have missed the program that would have taught them to fear human beings. In Darwin's words,

> The bay [of the islands] swarmed with animals: fish, shark and turtles popping their heads up in all parts. . . . These islands appear paradises for the whole family of reptiles. Besides three kinds of turtles, the tortoise is so abundant that a single ship's company caught 500–800 in a short time. The black lava rocks on the beach are frequented by large, most disgusting lizards [i.e., iguanas]. . . .
> The birds are strangers to man [yet] think him as innocent as their countrymen, the huge tortoises. Little birds, within three or four feet away, quietly hopped about the bushes and were not frightened.[11]

Almost 150 years later, Annie Dillard was similarly entranced by all that she saw at the Galapagos.

> These reptiles and insects, small animals and birds, evolved unmolested on the various islands on which they were cast into unique species adapted to the boulderwrecked shores. . . . You come for the animals. . . . You walk among the four-foot marine iguanas heaped on the shore lava, and on each other like slag. You swim with penguins; you watch flightless cormorants dance beside you, ignoring you. . . . Here are nesting blue-footed boobies. . . . The tortoises are as big as stones. The enormous land iguanas at your feet change color in the sunlight, from gold to blotchy red as you watch. . . .
> The animals are tame. . . . The marine iguanas are tame. . . . The wild hawk is tame. . . . In the Galapagos, even the flies are tame. . . . It all began in the Galapagos with the finches. The finches in the Galapagos are called Darwin's finches. . . . You stand on a flat of sand by a shallow lagoon rimmed in mangrove thickets and call the birds right out of the sky.[12]

The Galapagos Islands are attractive because they suggest a unity between the human world and the natural world, a friendly harmony among all that makes up God's created order. It is a harmony and unity sadly missing in the main thoroughfares of our modern life.

> To say that all life is an interconnected membrane, a weft of linkages like chainmail, is truism. But in this case . . . the Galapagos afford a clear picture.[13]

However romantic or utopian the tone of this chapter, let me assure you that the goal of our exploration will not be that of looking back (except to learn from the past), nor will it be to suggest that we simply regress to an earlier, sweeter stage of humankind's development (if such were possible). Rather it will be an exercise in looking at the signs of our times, examining the gathering clouds in the western sky, and praying that we can, with God's good grace, do our part to see that the storm blows over.

All of the religions of the world, in one way or another, are about right and harmonious relationships between humankind and the Divine Being, and relationships among people. The Summary of the Law states,

> You shall love the Lord your God with all your heart, with all your soul, and with all your mind. . . . You shall love your neighbor as yourself. On these two commandments hang all the Law and the Prophets.[14]

The summary bespeaks of the relationship (love) between God and God's people and of relationship among people (love). The Hebrew Scriptures set the foundations for the relationship between people and the environment as well as the consequences that will ensure if God's children fail to honor that relationship (note especially Deuteronomy 8). As churches have developed historically, however, the environmental teachings of our biblical tradition have been largely ignored, for we have been reluctant to extend just and loving relationships to include respect, love, and care for *all* aspects of life on our planet. The formulation of such an ethic is more than timely, for the fact remains that Creation is not yet finished. God created the world; God continues to create the world; God continues to act through those who have been created. Creation is not a word ending with a period; rather, it is an ongoing dynamic process in which all things continue to be made and to be made anew. This is the reason why we can with confidence sing the words of the hymn writer Charles Wesley: "*Finish* then thy new creation."[15]

Inspired both by Scripture and by the telling signs in God's Creation, as well as the sign of God's fallen Creation and its consequences, we will attempt to cast the net even further, to include all of the natural world so that we may take a fresh look at what it may mean to take care of God's old Creation and build on it a renewed one of fair and cordial relations with all of the marvelous works and wonders of earth, sea, and sky.

In the immediate aftermath of World War II, fresh with the memory of those fateful August days of 1945 during which thousands of Japanese civilians were killed and injured in two separate bombings, Jewish theologian Martin Buber was filled with foreboding. If human beings were capable of that much destruction of people and property, to say nothing of the horrors of Nazi gas chambers, Creation must be at the brink of unmitigated disaster. Buber expressed it as follows:

> For the last three decades we have felt that we were living in the initial phases of the greatest crisis humanity has ever known. It grows increasingly clear to us that the tremendous happenings of the past years can be understood as symptoms of this crisis. It is not one economic and social system being suspended by another, more or less ready to take its place; rather all systems, old and new, are equally involved in the crisis. What is in question, therefore, is nothing less than [humankind's] whole existence in the world.[16]

As a people we have become very good at looking at ourselves. It is not for nothing that ours has been termed the "Me Generation," living in what Christopher Lasch has called "the culture of narcissism." What I want, what I am, what I can do, what I need, what I have become, what I can be, what I have—I. Nor have those who profess to be religious been unaffected by the me-ness of our age. My God, my awareness, my pilgrimage of faith, my calling, my ministry—my.

I, me, my people have brought humankind and natural-kind to the crossroads, to the brink of the abyss, to the present about which Jonathan Schell said, "Everything we do and everything we are is in jeopardy."[17]

And there is another danger, this one internal, that in another way may be as threatening as the external danger of nuclear holocaust to which Buber and Schell refer: We as a people are rotting at the core; we are decaying and falling apart from the inside. It doesn't matter how many warheads the Russians—or anyone else, for that matter—have aimed at our shores; we are already killing ourselves by ourselves, without any outside assistance. Perhaps it is a slow killing, but it is a killing nonetheless. The paradox is that we have loved ourselves and what we have perceived as good for us (our health, our diets, our exercise, our work, our possessions, our accomplishments, our country, our churches, and, yes, even our intimate relationships) so much that a poison has entered into our love. That poison has harmed all of the above, and as a result, we are people who have lost our moral and ethical grounding. We have become an empty case, casting aimlessly about, as if swept along by a mighty wind—unanchored and drifting, unattached to the shore where Granny Dodge still lives her rooted, purposeful life.

*She stands as she has done for millennia, cutting bread, setting out sliced
vegetables on a plate, with a bottle of wine, and thinks that nothing in this
meal is safe, that the poisons of their civilization are in every mouthful, and
that they are about to fill their mouths with deaths of all kinds. In an instinctive
gesture of safety, renewal, she hands a piece of bread to her child, but
the gesture has lost its faith as she makes it, because of what she may be
handing the child.*

——Doris Lessing

2. The Rape of Creation

From Granny's Shore to Anne's Shore

It is with a twinge of sadness that we leave Granny Dodge on
her stable shore and begin to contemplate my own troubled shore.

A lovely brook tumbles over the rocks as it loses height and curls
its course around our house. We love the brook. We are drawn to
it, and I cannot explain just why. We moved here partly because
we wanted to live close to the brook. At the time we sensed that we
would feel nurtured by its fresh appearance and the rhythm of its
flow, and it has been so. As I write these pages the brook's steady
sound is there in the background, and I am indeed nurtured by it.

Spring rains swell the brook, and the sound of its rushing waters
closes out the rumble of the distant traffic. In the wintertime I know
I have to wrap up extra warmly if I see that ice has formed over its
surface. In the summer the brook still flows, even though it is a thinner,
slower brook.

At every season the water is sparklingly clear. Through it the
mica-splashed stones glitter in the afternoon sun. And always the
pine trees, the oak, and elm trees grow very thickly at its edges. The
ferns, the moss, and all the little shrubs are strong and sturdy. They
are like the trees the psalmist refers to, "trees planted by streams
of water, bearing fruit in due season with leaves that do not wither;
everything they do shall prosper" (Ps. 1:3).

On the far side of the brook is a huge rock. We call it the
"meditation rock," and on occasion we sit on it and just watch

the water roll by, feeling the irrepressible urge to let loose and shout with the psalmist, "Let the rivers clap their hands, and let the hills ring out with joy before the Lord" (Ps. 98:8).

But all is not completely well in this domestic Garden of Eden, for at times in the corners of the brook there is gathered a mysterious-looking, foamy white mass, a sort of liquid cotton candy. I wonder what this is. The water flowing over the rocks appears to be clean and clear, but still this foamy mass builds up. I wonder what is upstream that could be causing it, and I am uneasy.

This is but a small reminder of the many ways apart from, but also related to, our nuclear madness that the quality of our life and the quality of our environment are deteriorating. Opening our eyes for a full view, each one of us will see the instances in which we are directly affected by the deterioration. And we will also observe how the environmental deterioration that affects us personally is merely a part of a whole web of interlocking connections—a kind of cause-and-effect cosmos.

Nuclear Nightmare

The day began just like any other—the summer sun shone brilliantly on the bone-dry New Mexico desert, and there was a clear view for miles in every direction. But July 16, 1945, at Alamagordo, New Mexico, was destined to be a different day, long to be remembered, for just a few miles away at the Trinity Test Site, the first atomic bomb was detonated, ushering humankind abruptly into the Nuclear Age. At the time, no one noted the irony in the religious name of the test site—Trinity—but everyone at the outer edge of the site only too readily noticed that even with eyes tightly closed and hands cupped over them for protection, they could still see every bone in their fingers perfectly outlined the moment the atomic fire was ignited. This was an instant X ray like no other. This was fire beyond anyone's wildest imagining—a primal element gone berzerk. The awe of the blast so impressed one of the generals who was there that he described it this way:

> The whole country was lighted by a searing light with an intensity many times brighter than the midday sun. . . . Thirty seconds after the explosion came, first an air blast pressing hard against people and things, to be followed almost immediately by a strong, substantial, awesome roar which warned of doomsday and made us feel that we puny things were blasphemous to dare tamper with the forces heretofore reserved to the Almighty.[1]

This was a fire at one and the same time both alluring and repelling. But it was more alluring than repelling, particularly for the top military brass who were thousands of miles away, either behind Pacific bunkers or in the safety of sterile Pentagon offices, for in less than a month they gave the nod to the weapons wizards to do it again. Somehow it didn't seem to matter that Japan was on the verge of surrender anyway or that General Eisenhower and Admiral William Leahy, head of the Joint Chiefs of Staff, opposed the use of the bomb, for on August 6, 1945, the explosion of an atomic bomb at Hiroshima killed upward of 130,000 men, women, and children. Three days later another 75,000 people were killed and wounded when a second Japanese city—Nagasaki—was struck, this time with a plutonium bomb.

Not to be outdone by the bellicose Americans, physicists in the U.S.S.R., Great Britain, France, China, and India repaired to their laboratories, where they feverishly experimented and prepared for the time when they, too, would have their own tools of terror.

And now, even though the Nuclear Age is over forty years on— just coming into middle age, one might say—the world has yet to experience a global thermonuclear war. But we have come close on several occasions, and, during the intervening time, the United States and the Soviet Union have invented an ominous new Nuclear Age spectator sport. It is a spectator sport because, just as in any big league game, only a few are players or stars, their coaches, backups, and support systems; and then there are all the rest of us whose only role is to observe the action from the sidelines, essentially powerless to participate. Describing this as the action-reaction cycle, Arthur Laffin has documented the race in an essay in his book, *Swords Into Plowshares:*

> The United States was the first to develop the atomic bomb, the hydrogen bomb, the intercontinental bomber, the submarine-launched ballistic missile (SLBM), the multiple independently targeted re-entry vehicle (MIRV), the maneuverable re-entry vehicle (MARV), and the new cruise, Pershing II, MX, and Trident missiles.[2]

The 1986 Annual Report of General Dynamics boasts of the fact that new Trident submarines will be fitted with Trident II (D-5) missiles and that they also anticipate the refitting of the original eight Tridents with D-5 capability between 1991 and 1997.[3] One Trident submarine, equipped with twenty-four Trident II (D-5) missiles, *each* of which can travel 6,000 nautical miles and come within 300 feet of its target, would be able to destroy 192 targets with a blast exceeding that of 7,000 Hiroshimas.[4]

The Soviets, for their part, have responded with the development of comparable weapons. Again, to quote Laffin:

> The Soviets first developed the intercontinental ballistic missile system

(ICBM) in 1957 and the anti-ballistic missile system (ABM) in 1968. In response the United States developed an ICBM in 1958 and an ABM in 1972.[5]

True, in 1987 President Reagan and General Secretary Gorbachev signed the Intermediate Nuclear Force (INF) Treaty agreeing to the removal of 1,565 Soviet and 348 U.S. land-launched nuclear missiles. But lurking in the background shadow of the historic Reagan-Gorbachev talks was the knowledge that actually both the U.S.A. and the U.S.S.R. are rapidly shifting the locations of the majority of their strategic warheads to submarines[6] (thus lessening reliance on ground-based missiles) and that they are both engaged in research and a development of a Star Wars system, a so-called nuclear shield, which is expected to repell one or the other's nuclear warhead before it reaches its target.

In order to bring some perspective to the stark reality of the meaning of weapons, just try to imagine that an average warhead contains a yield of 2 million tons of TNT and that 2 million tons of TNT is about equivalent to all the bombs exploded during all of World War II.[7] This is the power of *just one bomb*. Now multiply it by 50,000—the number of nuclear weapons that are estimated to be in the arsenals of the world.

What is the human cost of this deadly U.S.-U.S.S.R. nuclear arms marathon—without so much as one bomb yet having been dropped on either country? Global military spending in 1986 was $900 billion.[8] This figure, according to the United Nations–sponsored report, *Our Common Future,* written by the World Commission on Environment and Development (WCED), is more than the *total income* of the poorest half of humanity, representing almost $1,000 for every one of the world's one billion poorest persons. Or, stated somewhat differently, that $900 billion in military spending in one year exceeded the combined gross national products of China, India, and the African countries south of the Sahara for the same year.[9]

The United States' share of worldwide military spending has been about one third of the total amount. In fact, since World War II, the United States has spent over $2,800,000,000,000 (almost $3 trillion) for military purposes.[10] According to the Committee for a Sane Nuclear Policy, the price tags for specific armaments are as follows: B-1 bombers—$6.9 billion; MX missiles—$6.6 billion; nuclear fast-attack submarines—$2.2 billion; M-1 tank—$1.9 billion; and Pershing II missiles—$500 million.[11] (Some of these items are currently slated for dismantling.) The Air Force's B-2 Stealth bomber, currently being developed, is expected to cost between $515 million and $568 million for *each plane.*[12] At the *same time* that funds for the above-listed armaments were being requested for the Pentagon budget, budgetary cuts in the following areas were also being proposed: energy, natural resources, and the environment—$3.2 billion; rural housing—$3.1 billion; nine programs affecting low-income people, including food stamps, energy assistance, and aid to families with dependent children—$4.1 billion; education, training, and social services—$2.2 billion; medical care for the needy—$1.7 billion; and mass transit—$590 million.[13]

Bringing this closer to home, to my home state of Connecticut: Connecticut's total contribution to the military spending for 1986 was $7.1 billion, which can be translated into $2,250 for every man, woman, and child in the state.[14]

Far more distressing than actual financial costs of the nuclear arms marathon are the severe tolls taken in human life. There are already as estimated 16 million innocent victims of radioactive fallout from nuclear testing.[15] Some of them have passed on genetic damage to generations yet unborn, and others have developed thyroid nodules and other medical problems.[16]

And there are other human costs: Making comparisons between global arms expenditurers and the funds *not spent* on health care, nutrition, education, and housing is a sobering exercise because the figures indicate our national priorities. As Ruth Sivard has illustrated, both military and social programs are obliged to compete for a share of the limited amount of national resources, and

> the goal of maximizing military power can be pursued only at the expense of other goals which are also essential to the common security. . . . Through the myriad of links that now tie nation to nation, it also affects global progress, and the kind of life each of us, especially the poorest and weakest among us, will be able to live.[17]

Bennett and George, in their study of global hunger, have made the point that the same amount now being spent *every two weeks* by the nations of the world on armaments would be enough to provide adequate food, water, education, health care, and housing for every person on earth for a year.[18] Furthermore, the countries that can least afford these vast sums—the developing nations that cannot adequately feed their burgeoning populations as it is—are spending some $7.2 billion a year on imported armaments. Argentina, for example, used French-manufactured Exocet missiles in the war over the Falkland Islands in 1982. Ethiopia used sophisticated Soviet MIG-21 fighters in its internal war,[19] while at the very same time, the starving victims of that country's drought were on nightly display on major television network newscasts. American-made Stinger missiles were the weapons of choice for Afganistan mountain soldiers in their war with the Soviets.[20]

Far more than a bomb was launched that fateful day forty years ago on the New Mexico desert. Launched also were the dreams of building a peacetime nuclear world. Soldiers and military engineers were joined by statesmen, business leaders, and politicians in sharing that dream. Illusions abounded about the wonderful possibilities of the newly discovered cheap energy. Although Dwight Eisenhower, by this time president, may initially have been skeptical about nuclear power, he soon changed his tune under the pressure of the business community, and in 1953 he launched a new public relations approach to nuclear power: Atoms for Peace. Every school room in the United States displayed futuristic posters depicting the splitting of the atom. Eisenhower's celebrated Atoms for Peace speech, translated into ten languages, captured the front pages of virtually every American and foreign newspaper.[21] All kinds of claims were being made: atoms could power ships (the first nuclear-powered submarine was in fact delivered in 1955); they could provide the power for whole cities inexpensively; they could even cure illnesses. At the same time a shroud of secrecy was dropped over the nuclear enterprise. The Atomic Energy Commission was giving away no secrets, especially those about the dark side of nuclear energy—the harmful effects to people and to the environment.

While Atoms for Peace was benefiting from an enormously successful publicity campaign (and the unpeaceful, unhealthy aspects of the Nuclear Age hushed up), nuclear power for both military and civilian purposes continued to be developed—mostly in parts of the world that were out of sight and out of sound of the great majority of the populace, such as in remote desert lands and on Pacific atolls inhabited by native people. Between 1945 and 1984 no fewer than 1,522 nuclear test explosions were conducted in the Pacific.[22] Only within the last two decades have the horror stories begun to emerge from other remote locations: the death of sheep, cattle, and Navajo Indians in the Southwest, for example. The British tests carried out in Australia and on the colonial islands of the Pacific in the early 1950s included the Totem Bomb detonated at Emu, which exposed an unwitting band of aboriginal people one hundred miles downwind of the explosion to vomiting and blinding as eighty rems of radiation enveloped them in a sinister "black mist."[23] British and Australian pilots flying through the radioactive cloud were somewhat less affected but affected nonetheless. It took until the early 1980s to assemble the data about their cancers, birth defects, and cataracts, which developed as a result of the Totem test.[24] Then there have been the French tests at Mururoa Atoll in French Polynesia that have continued relentlessly despite two decades worth of protests and two major accidents plus the blowing up of the Greenpeace ship (by the French secret service) in a New Zealand harbor in 1985. Thus, there is a reason that the Pacific Ocean has been called the "backyard of the nuclear arms race" and that the region has the highest rate of species extinction in the world.[25]

To some, the bikini is a glamorous and alluring style of bathing suit. But Bikini—the Pacific atoll after which the suit is named—is neither glamorous nor alluring. In 1946 when Bikini and Enewetak were selected for the first American nuclear tests in the Pacific, the people who lived there were told that the U.S. was testing nuclear bombs "for the good of mankind and to end all world wars."[26] Thus it was that the 166 residents of the two atolls were "asked" to leave—becoming the world's first "nuclear nomads." They were first evacuated to an uninhabited atoll, Rongerik, given two weeks' supply of food, and forgotten. Two years later, an American health care worker who visited the hapless nuclear nomads at Rongerik declared that they were "on the verge of starvation."[27] The Bikinians were starving and dying from the tremendous disruption in their lives and from broken hearts—not radiation sickness.

Thus was not the case for the residents of Rongelap, another of the Marshall Islands. The Rongelapians were awakened one spring morning in 1954 by a blinding flash of light to the west—a light as bright as the sun that was followed by a thunderous explosion that shook at the foundations of the islands. By afternoon a two-inch layer of "snowlike" ash had settled on the ground. Not knowing the nature of this strange visitation, the people walked through it, children played in it, tossing it merrily in the air as it continued to fall well on into the night. The ash became yellow as it settled into the drinking water, and by bedtime the people had begun to feel nauseous, and their skin itched all over.[28] A Marshallese man who was there described the bewildering occurance (adapted):

> That yellow dust started to fall here on Rongelap and we wondered.
> . . . The plane circled around and some say it dropped dust. Some say
> to kill mosquitos. . . . And many set out basins and wash tubs to collect
> the dust and save it. All the children were running between the houses
> and playing with the dust. Something new for them. But by evening they
> started to get sick. That is when they started to say—maybe dust is
> poison! And that night came rain and the powder washed down roofs
> into cisterns and the next morning all the people were throwing up and
> thirsty and many drank that water. . . . Then everyone came together
> at the church. All children and everyone came to pray. All the people
> were sick and wondered what was happening to them.[29]

The strange visitation was the fallout from Bravo—then the largest U.S. hydrogen bomb—a warhead one thousand times more powerful than the Hiroshima bomb. In addition to the Rongelapians, other innocent victims were affected by the blast: 23 Japanese fishermen on board the "Lucky Dragon," 28 Americans at a neighboring weather station on Rongerik Atoll, and 157 Marshallese on Utrik Atoll.

Some of these innocents died of radiation sickness shortly after the hit; others developed their symptoms slowly—miscarriages, stillbirths, thyroid tumors, leukemia. Over the years some 69 percent of the children who were age ten or younger at the time of the Bravo test developed thyroid tumors.[30] Why hadn't the people been warned of the test and evacuated? The Marshallese had always felt that this was quite deliberate and that they were being used as guinea pigs in order to provide the Americans an opportunity to test the effects of radiation on human beings. In fact, almost thirty years later a United States Defense Nuclear Agency report confirmed these suspicions. The lack of warning was no accident.[31]

Turning for a moment from the harmful effects of radiation on people, let us touch lightly of the destruction of the land: Nuclear debris has contaminated Bikini and Einewetak as well as the French atoll of Mururoa in French Polynesia for an estimated several thousand years into the future. The residents of the affected Marshall Islands tried to return to their homes, but when they began to develop radiation illness again, they were forced to resume their nomadic state. And now forty years after the beginning of the first nuclear tests, hardly an issue of the weekly *Marshall Islands Journal* comes out without an article about the settlement of health and land damage claims. And the Marshallese have been joined by many more nuclear nomads who have had to flee other contaminated areas on other continents and other nuclear ghost towns.

The areas surrounding some civilian nuclear plants have been similarly—if less dramatically—damaged. Britain's Windscale nuclear installation (now called Sellafield) is an example. Windscale has acquired the dubious reputation of being the world's worst plant for dangerous radioactive discharges.[32] As a result of its various radioactive emissions, leaks, and such, a quarter of a ton of plutonium now rests at the bottom of the Irish Sea, making that body of water the most radioactive sea in the world.[33] It took a fire that blazed out of control for forty-two hours in one of the plant's reactors and twenty deaths to finally close down Windscale. And before the story ends on the calamities of Windscale, 260 people who were living in the vicinity are likely to develop thyroid cancer. Hundreds of square miles have been so heavily contaminated by radioactive wastes that most of the area is now forbidden territory and the burned-out reactor remains entombed in concrete, an ugly and dangerous scar on the land.[34]

The March 1979 near meltdown at the Three Mile Island nuclear power plant in Pennsylvania has caused a great deal of anxiety to people in the surrounding area, and it confirmed their fears that the worst can occur. Indeed, it did so in what was once a pretty farming community in Russia. It took the Chernobyl accident in the Ukraine in April 1986 to bring home to the world in practical ways the fact that atoms—even so-called peaceful ones—can become matters of grave international concern. In northern Europe where national boundaries are close together, Chernobyl demonstrated that no nuclear castrophe can necessarily be expected to be contained within national borders and that an ill wind of radioactive fallout can bring hardship to unwitting people many miles away from an accident site, in addition to making a modern ghost town of the accident site. How does one explain to the Lapland hunter, for instance, that the deer he has shot for his family (the deer that has been grazing on grass contaminated by fallout) may just do his family in or that the milk he gives his little ones to drink might be a slow-acting poison?

But suppose no nuclear plant ever had an accident, we are still left with the problem of the disposal of the waste from nuclear reactors. Naturally, given the choice, no one wants a radioactive dump in their locale, yet the nation's few hazardous waste dumps are rapidly filling up. There are very few locations that qualify as safe dumping sites because a dump cannot be placed near a population center or an underground aquifer or a river. Indeed, since 1975 the United States Energy Research and Development Administration has been hard at work looking for a new site for 77,000 tons of radioactive waste. Palmyra Island in the Pacific has been on the list, also Deaf Smith County in Texas, and Hanford, Washington. Yucca Mountain in Nevada is now the prime candidate.[35]

Toxic waste is quickly becoming a desperate problem. Understandably, no one with any say in the matter wants nuclear refuse anywhere near them. Bleakly one realizes that Third World nations are becoming repositories of First World waste. Many shipfuls of toxic waste, for example, had already been deposited in the world's poorest nations before Nigeria refused to receive Italy's 2,100 tons of nuclear refuse aboard the Karin B. The environmental organization Greenpeace recently reported that, in the last two years, First World countries exported 3.6 million tons of toxic waste, most of it to Africa and Caribbean nations.[36] The Marshall Islands are next: An American waste disposal firm, Admiralty Pacific, is getting ready to bring tons of garbage to the Marshalls beginning in June 1990. Twenty pounds of each ton exported is expected to be toxic. Ultimately it is intended that 10 percent of all refuse produced on the West Coast of the United States will find its final resting place in the Marshall Islands.[37]

Truly God's people and God's land are being wasted while the world is held hostage by nuclear "experts" who have neither respect for God's people nor loving consideration for God's environment.

And finally there is the waste of the time and imagination that might otherwise be utilized on ventures to build up the human community. In 1985, it was estimated that one scientist and one engineer out of every four were being employed in the devising and testing of weapons systems and that approximately 50 million people were variously employed in armaments industries.[38] Add to that number all the other millions of scientists, engineers, and technicians who are employed in civilian nuclear power industries throughout the world, as well as those in other nonnuclear yet environmentally harmful enterprises. Surely the diversion of this talent is in itself a waste of God's Creation. Even President Eisenhower, on reflecting upon this matter, was moved to conclude that

> every gun that is made, every warship launched, every rocket fired signifies, in the final sense, a theft from those who hunger and are not fed, those who are cold and not clothed. This world in arms is not spending money alone. It is spending the sweat of its laborers, the genius of its scientists, the hopes of its children. . . . This is not a way of life at all in any true sense. Under the cloud of threatening war, it is humanity hanging from a cross of iron.[39]

Unfortunately, it takes a Chernobyl or a Bikini to alert the general public to the death, disease, and destruction of people and the planet that is going on everyday, everywhere, wholescale and unchecked.

All things considered, all aspects of God's created order are at risk, and it all began at a test site called Trinity on a parched and barren desert in New Mexico. So much for Atoms for Peace. Just look what peaceful atoms have done for us!

Surely, God looks over all that he created, and behold, he weeps.

Unease Up Close

For myself, I start with my shore and the brook with its curious foamy mass. Our well lies about five hundred feet from the brook. It is a shallow "dug well" as they call it, making it more vulnerable to pollutants than a deeply drilled well. A drilled well would have been deeper, safer. We are one of the million households in Connecticut that rely on wells for our domestic water supply. We are now learning that we are vulnerable no matter what our well type is. As early as a decade ago, regional water authorities considered that chemicals, toxic wastes, pesticides, and various industrial pollutants would not reach the ground water that is trapped in low-lying sand and gravel. But lo and behold, that ground water, so recently deemed safe, is now being affected. In the town of North Madison, not far from us, Andrea Woods has noticed that her well water sometimes smells oily. "When my husband changes the oil in the car, it smells a lot like that."[40] The Woods family has switched to bottled water, and so have 150,000 other Connecticut house-holders. The cause of the contaminated North Madison water supply is leaking underground gasoline storage tanks containing a carcino-genic additive. This makes me wonder. What is the cause of the white foam in our brook? In the next town over there is a nuclear waste-storage dump for "low radiation" refuse. Is the runoff from that dump leaking into the brook? More to the point, less than a quarter of a mile away from me is the resevoir that is the main water source for the city of New London, our county seat, with a population of 29,000. If a small brook can be affected and the wells of a thousand households, what about the contaminants that seep into this and the other resevoirs in the state? Nationally, it has been estimated that the water supply affecting 34 million households is in one way or another contaminated.[41] It does not take much imagination to understand why supermarkets are doing a brisk trade in bottled water.

From ground water and drinking water, the mind moves on to ocean water. Every summer the snapper blues—baby bluefish—run along the beaches and stony outcroppings of the Long Island Sound. They ride in on the incoming tide, sometimes in such abun-dance that every cast of the line will bring in a fish. When my sons were boys they spent many a lazy August afternoon catching the little fish, which provided a delectable and free supper for the family. Our fish supper nights were high points of the summer—until we began to notice a mild scent of motor oil as we opened up the fish and cleaned them in preparation for the meal. Now a decade later, long after the boys stopped putting fresh fish on the dinner table, the documentation on the health risk has emerged. A 1987 report of the National Marine Fisheries Service surveying bluefish along the coastline from New England to Florida found dangerously high PCB (toxic polychlorinated biphenyl) levels in one of every six of the larger fish. Our area, known as the New York Bight (the 4,500 square mile expanse running from Cape May, New Jersey, to Montauk Point at the end of Long Island), is the worst with 45 percent of the fish tested proving unsafe.[42]

Perhaps it isn't so bad that we cannot eat the fish the Rowthorn brothers catch. After all, they just fished recreationally. But what about the scores of Connecticut's poor who have always depended upon a few tasty and free summer fish frys? Or what about those who make their living by working in the fishing industry? The area around New Bedford harbor in Massachusetts is so polluted it is now closed to commercial fishing, and Maine's $11 million-a-year clam industry is also threatened.[43]

It turned out to be a disillusioning occasion the first time I saw Lake Michigan. It was the first of the Great Lakes I had seen, and I will never forget the experience. We were camping at Indiana Dunes State Park behind the bluffs. The lake was a quarter of a mile away from the campground. The trail to it wound around scraggy, windswept evergreen trees to a hill overlooking the lake. Below was the beach with beautiful, clean, white sand lining the border. Looking ahead toward the horizon was water as far as the eye could carry. To the left were the smokestacks of Gary and beyond them the skyscrapers of the great city of Chicago. The air was perfectly clear and the panoramic view from the crest of the hill where we stood was nothing short of spectacular. Then we descended the trail through the dunes to the beach. We could not wait to get there as we eagerly anticipated enjoying the shore and the water up close and taking a cool, refreshing swim in it. But as we got closer we noticed that the water's edge was dotted with something we had not seen from the hill above, something emitting a foul odor. This puzzled us, but not for long. We were soon to discover that the beach was dotted with the corpses of 10,000 decaying fish, all lying on their sides with drying skins and open mouths. Oddly, one would also have expected flies, but there were none, perhaps because a fresh wind was blowing off the lake. So much for a first encounter with one of our nation's greatest lakes.

More disillusioning than dead fish is the phenomena of no fish at all in an area where they were once plentiful. The reality of this no-fish situation is new, and new is our understanding of hypoxia. Hypoxia is a condition caused by decomposing sewage acting in conjunction with waste nutrients like phosphorus and nitrogen. The action works by consuming oxygen, which results in a depletion of the oxygen required by marine animals to breathe—to have life. So hypoxia is like a giant, uncontrolled ocean cancer, destroying healthy marine life as it stimulates a negative process of decay and death. Hypoxia's only product is an ugly, dull brown algae; it is an algae that has already wiped out the $1.8 million scallop industry in one Long Island town and eliminated small fin fish as well.[44] The 12 million people who live in the vicinity of the Long Island Sound are affected by the lifeless, polluted ocean water; so also are local waterfowl and migratory birds whose flight patterns take them over the Sound to feed and then on to spread the contamination to other areas.

The deadening of our waters and the contamination of our fish are signs that "the chickens have come home to roost," that our disrespect for the environment is having consequences. The results of our irresponsible actions may be slow in coming to light, but they are emerging and coming to our attention nonetheless. Like radiation sickness, manifestations of disease may be slow in showing up, but it is just a matter of time. For generations we have regarded the oceans as ideal dumping grounds for all manner of chemical, nuclear, and industrial wastes. In the New York Bight alone, *every year* some 800 billion gallons of sewage are discharged containing bacteria, viruses, and chemicals; 150 industries dump 150,000 gallons of acid wastes in deep-sea dumping grounds; forty-nine tons of wood debris are burned every year.[45] Added to this are the emissions of nuclear power plants, which are purposely situated beside waterways since they require millions of gallons of water every day to cool their systems. We do not yet know what the combined long-term effects of radiation *and* chemical pollutants will be on human beings, but we do know that areas surrounding nuclear plants have fewer fish, less lobster larvae and plankton.[46]

And speaking of nuclear power plants, what about the ones close to home? It was enlightening to me to move to eastern Connecticut, to the country, to live in a home in the woods on the edge of a sparkling (but possibly contaminated) brook and find that the yellow pages of the local telephone directory contain no information as to how I might contact local legislators but three pages of finely detailed emergency instructions as to what to do in case of a nuclear power accident. There are four nuclear power plants in our area (one complex that contains three of them is descriptively called Millstone), and there are four relocation centers with maps and routes to them carefully laid out for the ten-mile radius of each plant. I am even informed that I can preregister at the local civil preparedness office if I have "special needs" (elderly, disabled, etc.) and, if I were a parent, that I need not worry because, during school hours, the children will be transported directly from the school to our area relocation center. The evacuation plans are all worked out in efficient and chilling detail along with the comforting information graciously supplied by the Millstone Energy Center that, after all, even if I lived right next door to a nuclear power plant, my family would only be exposed to one millirem of radiation a year—far safer, it is pointed out, than a chest X-ray, smoking two packs of cigarettes a day, or just going out in the sun (the latter will give one 40 millirems of radiation a year).[47] But, in fact, all four of the plants have been cited for safety violations. One of them is on the list of the nation's twenty-five worst plants in terms of workers' exposure to radiation.[48] At the other plants, employees' reports of safety violations submitted to the Nuclear Regulatory Commission (NRC) have resulted in harassment by plant higher-ups.[49] A member of a church two miles from Millstone offered me her brand of comfort, or was it a rationalization? She told me that, actually, we who live close to the power station are the fortunate ones. We will die quickly, being spared the slow agony of radiation sickness and decline into death. While such a sanguine approach does not sit well with me, I must admit that the reality of living so close to the nuclear power stations and hardly giving them a thought from one week to the next is just one more example of how much I have become adapted to a diminished quality of everyday life.

The sun as source of all life is deeply embedded in archaic mythology. Inti, the sun, was the imperial god of the Incas. Every Inca province accorded a privileged place to the sun. The Temple of the Sun at Cuzco was an edifice of great magnificence and importance, on a par with Solomon's Temple to the Jews. The Aztecs were popularly known as "the People of the Sun." In Aztec mythology, earth is mother; the sun, father. Sun and rain, fire and water—these are the great forces that rule the world. Preeminent is the sun, source and sustainer of all and worthy of all worship. But the sun, the source, may be killing us. Not because it in itself is dangerous, but because humankind, human ingenuity, has tampered with the invisible shield that has—as it were—kept the god at bay. That shield, ozone, serves as a protective screen, a gentle blanket that surrounds the planet and blocks out harmful ultraviolet radiation. Global ozone levels have dropped dramatically—by some estimates, as much as 5 percent—between the years 1979 and 1986. Scientists have been measuring ozone levels for a number of years. In the summer of 1987 they discovered a huge puncture in the ozone layer over Antarctica that caused some alarm because of the dimensions of the hole. In early 1988 they determined that ozone levels in the range of thirty degrees to sixty degrees north latitude had also been seriously affected. This area includes the heavily populated regions of the United States and Canada, western Europe, the Soviet Union, China, and Japan.[50] Practically speaking, each percentage point of ozone loss results in a 5 percent increase in the incidence of skin cancer among the general population. Now I worry about this because in the immediate sense already two of the light-skinned members of my family have been diagnosed with precancerous skin conditions.

What has caused this ozone depletion in the atmosphere? What has put us at risk? It is chlorofluorocarbons (CFCs)—industrial chemicals used in refrigeration, styrofoams, and aerosol sprays, also plastic foams and solvents—the by-products of our technological age. While it is no small achievement that we have been able to keep food fresh through freezing and refrigeration, there have been costs and the very source of life has become the agent of disease.

Ozone levels have been depleted in the upper stratosphere, while at the same time all types of pollutants have increased, trapping harmful gases at ground levels and contributing to the global warming trend we have come to call the "greenhouse effect." The greenhouse effect is more than a hot, unpleasant summer—it is the gradual warming some scientists have predicted will continue to raise average temperatures by three to nine degrees Farenheit by as early as the year 2030.[51] While there is as yet no irrefutable proof that global warming has begun, four of the past eight summers have been the warmest recorded in this century.[52] These increasing temperatures, if unchecked, will escalate the melting of polar ice caps, which could, before long, raise sea levels and put many coastal areas under water and at the same time increase drought episodes in arid areas, including the drying up of inland water sources.[53] Carbon dioxide emissions are the main cause of the greenhouse effect, mostly emissions caused by the combustion of fossil fuels—coal, oil, gas, and wood.[54] The rustic wood-burning stove is no friend of the environment.

Ironically, as we learn more about the greenhouse effect, the nuclear power industry may be given an unexpected boost since nuclear power produces virtually no greenhouse gases, neither carbon dioxide nor the gases that form acid rain.

So much for Father Sun and heat and pollution. And now Mother Earth. I have just returned from a trip to America's heartland. I drove a thousand miles around the back roads in the farming counties of rural Illinois and Missouri. Everywhere new spring life was beginning to burst into flower. Farmers were plowing up the rich black soil, row upon row of it for as many miles in every direction that the eye could see and the mind comprehend. The great American farm has fed the world, and it has nurtured me all my life. As it has provided food for city dining tables, it has filled me with images of health, wholeness, and well-being. As a child I wandered over the rangeland of the Dakotas, Montana, and Wyoming, marveling at the wonder of so much sky and the herds in their thousands upon the range. The tidy farm houses and barns of Kansas, Illinois, and Missouri gave me a happy feeling of contentment. All of these scenes, all of these images, filled me with a sense of the rightness of God's Creation. Surely the earth is good; surely amidst such abundance I have come to understand in my heart the notion of God's Creation praising God the Creator as the words in the Song of the Three Young Men (vss. 4, 34, 52, 54, 67) fall upon my lips and I sing out,

> All your works are true and your ways are right. . . .
> Blessed are you in the firmament of heaven and to be sung and
>   glorified for ever. . . .
> Let the earth bless the Lord; let it sing praise to him and highly
>   exalt him for ever. . . .
> Give thanks to the Lord, for God is good, and his mercy
>   endures for ever.

I had not driven through the heartland for a few years, and this trip was decidedly different from all the others. True, all the fields are being carefully plowed as always in the spring. Certainly tractors have changed for the better. The simple umbrella shading the driver from the blistering midday sun has given way to an enclosed tinted-glass, air-conditioned cab. Certainly the plowing machinery dragged by the tractor covers a much wider expanse of field. No doubt it breaks down less often. But many of the once-spruce farmhouses are now in need of a fresh coat of paint; some of them have caved in with neglect; others have been abandoned altogether. Many of the barns have a dilapidated look to them. Farm yards, once full of children and the paraphenalia of youth—bicycles, swing sets, baseball bats and beach balls, pet cats and dogs—are now empty. The farmhouse, the barn, the farm yard now give one an eerie feeling. Are they not monuments to the quiet tragedy of what our age has done to the American farmer? Where there was once life and vitality, the laughter of children, there is now the silent memory of what once was.

These areas have been like cardiac patients living on borrowed time, kept alive by miracle drugs and heroic surgical procedures. Even at the best of times the lands beyond the hundredth meridian (that invisible line that cuts through the Dakotas, Kansas, and the Oklahoma and Texas panhandles) have always been high, dry, and treeless. But the invention of the diesel-driven centrifugal pump capable of raising eight hundred gallons of water a minute changed that bleak picture.[55] This powerful pump gave the precarious western lands the possibility of becoming green and lush, for it allowed farmers to reach down to the Ogallala Aquifer, which runs beneath the hundredth meridian, and the rich harvest of water trapped there since the Ice Ages. The water of the Ogallala Aquifer was free; all that was required was the pump to bring it up and self-propelling sprinklers to spread it out over the thirsty sown fields. Now the mining of Ogallala water is regulated, but unfortunately, regulation came too late. Now water that might have lasted a hundred years is running dry—ten thousand years of groundwater almost used up in less than half a century.[56]

The simple windmill-driven pumps that once provided water enough for countless family farms have long since been stilled. Now many self-propelled sprinklers that spanned the verdant fields like giant caterpillars are also grinding to a halt as the centrifugal pumps that supply them are pumping deeper and deeper only to bring up more and more gravel and mud and less and less water. But other tokens of our age have also appeared on the prairie landscape.

Amid the grain silos—those great cathedrals of the plains—have now sprung up cathedrals of a different kind, new monuments of metal in praise of the gods of metal. Whereas in every prairie town the old silos stand a hundred feet up as landmarks visible from miles around, the thousand missile silos that have quietly emerged in the same land are each hidden a hundred feet below the ground. These space-age silos have been gradually appearing amid the corn and wheat fields since the mid-1950s, like weeds growing in paradise. They are inconspicuous, generally placed far from the beaten track, down gravel roads, tucked into the corners of fields and pastureland. These missile silos are not obvious. They do not attract much attention. They look a little like natural gas installations —gauges, tanks, pipes, poles, concrete slabs—all enclosed behind chain link fences.

Taking the "show me" state of Missouri as an example, let us look at these new cathedrals of the plains. The lush Missouri farmland has lying beneath it a crop of 150 nuclear missile installations. Under each of the installations' concrete slabs is a 100-foot deep, vertical tunnel, a reinforced silo. Each silo contains two or three Minuteman or MX intercontinental ballistic missiles (ICBMs), each with two or three independently targeted nuclear warheads with yields of 170 to 350 kilotons—a hundred times more powerful than the Hiroshima bomb.[57] Each missile is carefully aimed at a strategic population center in the Soviet Union. These "launch facilities" are interconnected by cable to fifteen "launch centers," one for each "flight" of ten missiles. The launch centers are supervised twenty-four hours a day by Air Force Strategic Air Command officers, who are stationed in underground capsules ready to release their deadly payload with thirty seconds notice.[58] Montana, North and South Dakota, Wyoming, and Nebraska also have their crops of warheads in missile fields. In all, there are one thousand nuclear weapon silos scattered about in our Great Plains heartland. They are a part of what the Pentagon calls its "strategic triad" of nine thousand land-based, submarine-launched, and bomber-delivered nuclear warheads.[59]

The foregoing is my personal catalogue of horrors, my causes for unease. Taken individually, these environmental trends affecting me may seem insignificant. And taken alongside of those that affect the great majority of world citizens who do not happen to be middle-class North Americans, they certainly do not mean much. Or, considered another way, since I am so much affected and my case is in no way exceptional when placed in the world context, this ought to give us pause. Privileged though I and my ilk may be, I nonetheless look at the list: I am directly affected by unsafe drinking water, polluted oceans, the risks of living close to nuclear power plants, the offense of missile silos in the heartland, and the loss of the ozone shield. Just one of these factors, such as unsafe drinking water, may not be much to worry about. But the concern is not just about one factor; it is about all of them. But if these factors of concern are bad for those of privilege and of the middle class in the United States, they are terrible for the people of Haiti and the Sudan and Mexico City and Jakarta. Furthermore, all the environmental trends are interrelated. The distinguished German theologian, Jürgen Moltmann, expresses it well:

> This is really a crisis of the whole life system of the modern industrial world. It is a crisis which human beings have brought on themselves and their natural environment, and into which they are driving both themselves and the environment more and more deeply.
>   The living relationship of human societies to the natural environment has been lastingly—if not already irreparably—destroyed by human technologies for exploiting nature. . . . So when we talk about the ecological crisis of modern civilization, we can only mean a *crisis of the whole system* with all its part-systems, from the dying of the forests to the spread of neuroses, from the pollution of the seas and rivers to the nihilistic feeling about life which dominates so many people in our mass cities. [And] the destruction of the natural environment [has brought about] a destructive retroactive effect of the societies them-selves, evoking a loss of values and crisis of meaning.[60]

You have your own list, your own polluted brook that runs by the front door of your house, for we are all, each one of us, surrounded by subtle and not so subtle reminders that all is not well with the world. For some it might be the algae beginning to creep into the once-pristine Boundary Waters of Minnesota. Possibly it is the foul-smelling mineral mines on the outskirts of Gillette, Wyoming; the polluted and debris-filled ocean waters necessitating the closing beaches from New Jersey to Massachusetts and along the Gulf of Mexico; or the acid rain, which is killing vast stretches of Adirondack woodlands. Maybe it is the toxic automobile emissions, which turn the tender, spring green plants of New York City's Central Park to a dull gray-brown before summer is half through.

Sometimes when I walk along the beaches of Connecticut or

around the shore of my native Massachusetts, my mind sets to wandering, and I try to imagine what it was like before the European settlers arrived. Or, sitting in Riverside Park, high over the banks of the Hudson, I find myself thinking about what it was like when the Hudson was just a river, not the great river flowing around Manhattan's forest of skyscrapers. And I marvel at what we have done to ourselves and to our land. I shudder that we have cared so little about the land we are passing on to our children and to our childrens' children. I marvel at our greed and our self-destructiveness, and like Jeremiah weeping over the desolation of Jerusalem, I ask myself, "Is this the City we called the perfection of beauty, the joy of all the earth?" (Lam. 2:15b).

Rotting at the Core: Destruction of the Social Landscape

The defeat of six million Incas by a handful of Spanish conquistadores has been attributed to internal strife and dissention that preceded the arrival of the Spaniards. One wonders also about what was happening in Greek and Roman society before their decline and collapse. All were societies of great accomplishment, creativity, architectural and artistic advances. They were all cultures of ideas, action, and possibility. Yet they were all brought low. How much did each of them, in fact, self-destruct? And I wonder about ourselves. We can devise the best military protection money can buy; we can invent the most elaborate medical and surgical procedures to extend our life expectancy; we can come up with the most scientific diets and exercise programs to keep our bodies intact. We can, and we do all of this. Yet we are falling apart. We are like one large, shiny, delicious apple, one that looks good on the outside but is rotting at the core. We might as well forget about other nations' missiles aimed at our cities. We do not need the destructive force of outsiders, for we are destroying ourselves, by ourselves, with no help from others. We deny it wholesale, but death is all around us and in us, and we are—all of us—(unwittingly perhaps) involved in a sort of collective, self-directed cultural genocide. Octavio Paz expresses it well:

> Death enters into everything we undertake, and it is no longer a transition but a great gaping mouth that nothing can satisfy. The century of health, hygiene and contraceptives, miracle drugs and synthetic foods, is also the century of the concentration camp and the police state, Hiroshima and the murder story. [Yet] nobody thinks about death . . . because nobody lives a personal [and personally and socially responsible] life.[61]

Rampant teenage pregnancy, domestic violence, spousal and child abuse, the failure of marriage, addictions of all kinds, destructive sexual practices—all of these are, in one way or another, life denying; all are the results of aggression turned inward or toward those who are close. It is not difficult to understand. We see events that worry us in our society, circumstances and conditions, perhaps unspoken and not even in our conscious mind—whether it is the condition of our land or of our national politics, broad social issues, issues of our immediate communities or our workplaces. Most of us feel helpless and impotent to address them. We can flip the channel and click in another program, plug a fantasy film into the VCR, pull another beer from the refrigerator. But whatever we do, we cannot drown out the issues, we cannot make them go away, nor can we will away our deep-seated anxiety about the conditions of society that trouble us. Our issues are too complex; there does not appear to be a way to address them. We can hardly conceptualize them enough to even talk about them. The issues of our times hurt us; they cause us pain. Yet we cannot do what would come naturally. We cannot strike out and hit them. We cannot attack the source of our pain, or we don't think we can anyway. But we can strike out against something. We can hit ourselves and those around us, and we can even kill ourselves because we are within our own reach. All that pain, all that hurt, all that anxiety, all that frustration at being unable to strike the sources of the pain—it is a force that has to go somewhere, so we lash out at each other and at ourselves. *Eros* and *thantos*, life and death, are, after all, natural human tendencies. It is not for nothing that we pray in the Lord's Prayer, "Deliver us from evil"—the evil within as well as the evil without—or that historically the churches have devoted so much energy to the doctrine of Original Sin. What is Original Sin but the death-dealing forces within each one of us?

From a psychoanalytic point of view, Freud described humankind's natural drift into destructiveness, and he correlated it with an internal spiritual malignancy. Working with individuals, he did not study the broader social consequences of the death instinct, but others have taken up where Freud left off. Karl Menninger's 1938 study of suicide, *Man Against Himself,* is still a classic, and others, such as Rollo May[62], and Konrad Lorenz,[63] have studied suicide and hostility and their meaning in society.

There are times in our past during which our collective death instinct has gained the upper hand, and there have been (and are) cultures that have absorbed, sublimated, and transformed aggressive instincts in ways less dangerous than ours. Right now we are the victims of a fatal combination of forces that make our present time dangerous indeed and call the future of our species into question.

All manner of personal and social dis-eases (already listed) that are a part of ourselves and those close to us are serious diseases in themselves. They are also symptoms of a diseased society. They are the manifestations of a people who have lost their grounding and their direction, of a people who collectively have become, to use Graham Greene's phrase, a "burnt-out case." And perhaps the most serious manifestation of our "burnt-out case" condition is that we have become a people seemingly immune to the tragedy of our own destructiveness, creatures who have lost the art of how to *care deeply* and wholesomely for ourselves and most especially for the other.

This is a society in which homelessness has become a way of life. It is a society, once criticized by our European neighbors for spoiling its children, that will now tolerate, in New York City alone, the condition of 13,000 homeless children.[64]

Children living in shelters and welfare hotels, whole families residing in cars and sleeping on warm sidewalk grates in all of our cities; children closed out of decent educational opportunities because of their parents' poverty or race—these children are the innocent victims of our social dis-ease. The author of a study on adolescent violence predicted that in the next five years, one in every five adolescents will live at or below the poverty line.[65]

> Poverty means poor hygiene, increased adolescent pregnancy, more substance abuse, higher school dropout rates and more crime. Unless we start dealing with the *underlying causes* of adolescent health problems, we are simply providing Band-Aids.[66]

Up close in my own state, the Connecticut Commission on Children issued a report in 1987 that contained some sobering statistics documenting the relationship between children, their families, and poverty. In the decade between 1970 and 1980, the percentage of children living with both parents dropped by 10 percent; the percentage of female-headed households nearly doubled; and by 1990 one in four children will be living in female-headed homes (and these are the children most likely to be living in poverty).[67] These are the statistics for all groups, and they are arresting enough in themselves. For black and Hispanic children they are far worse: In 1980, one in two black children under the age of eighteen, and one in three Hispanic children were living in female-headed households (as distinct from one in eight white children.)[68] These children of cultural and racial minorities are not only affected by the feminization of poverty but also by racism. All this in the state that has the highest per capita income in the nation.

Furthermore, as Marian Wright Edelman of the Children's Defense Fund said,

> It's not just the 13 million poor children, or millions more in moderate-income families who are still child care poor, housing poor, and higher education poor, who must struggle to keep their foothold in the American dream and who are unsure about their futures. A growing number of privileged youths suffer from spiritual poverty affected by "affluenza."[69]

The symptoms include boredom, low self-esteem, lack of motivation. Family wealth insulates these children from challenge, risk, and consequence. Social scientists are finding many parallels between children of the urban rich and those of the urban poor in that they both suffer from absentee parents and easily available drugs, alcohol, and sex.[70]

What is painfully obvious is that the American way of life has become the American way of death for an increasing number of people: the slow death by hunger, neglect, malnutrition, poor health care, addictions, and *quick death by suicide*. Between the years of 1950 and 1980, suicides among the general population increased 100 percent.[71] During that same thirty-year period, suicides among the fifteen- to twenty-four-year-old group increased by 300 percent.[72]

Above my writing table I have the family photograph of Pat Wallace, Paul Hodel, and their little daughter, Katherine Elizabeth, born two months ago. Pat is a low-income-housing expert, and Paul runs the nonprofit, grass-roots peace education and action center he founded. They are solid people and leaders in their community. Like everyone else, they have had some rough times in their lives and a long wait to become parents; and like everyone else, they want the best for their child. They are thrilled with the joy of their new beginning—the beginning of this stage of their lives and the new beginning, the new hope and promise of their young one. "It is a wondrous, exhilarating experience to bring a new person into the world," Paul wrote, yet he continued as follows:

> As beautiful and endearing as she may be, she is also very delicate and completely dependent on us for all her basic survival needs: food, shelter, cleanliness, and general nurture. It's easy for us, her parents, to provide those and much more with the tremendous love we feel and want so much to give. But as people who are life-long activists as well as parents we are also acutely conscious of the work we need to do besides providing food and clean diapers.
> The year will be 2022 when my daughter reaches the age of 34, my age at the beginning of her new life. It is natural for parents to hope and expect that their children will grow to be adults and have the same or even better opportunities than they did. And yet I must confess I am very uncertain as to whether my daughter and indeed the entire earth

can possibly survive until 2022 given present political and environmental trends.[73]

The Global Rape of Creation

If it could be argued that our American way of life fostered love, care, and a hopeful anticipation of the future, it is possibly conceivable that we might find some justification for our system, which has gone a long way in destroying the environment, built up a nuclear arsenal that could end all of Creation in half an hour, which has witnessed the demise of social and family stability. But the case cannot be made. All that our Yankee ingenuity has succeeded in accomplishing is to put a question mark over the life of Paul and Pat's little child and over the future of us all. And, it must be said, we are not only robbing our own children of their future, we are robbing the future and the *present* from people of the developing world. Economists such as Ruth Legar Sivard, the members of the United Nations World Commission on Environment and Development, and others have amply illustrated the relationship between Third World poverty and global trade, investment, and financial systems that favor northern capitalist-industrial nations at the expense of southern Third World nations. According to World Bank statistics, the gross national product (GNP) per capita in the United States is $11,500 compared with only $755 for countries of the south (i.e., Third World).[74] Yet the 70 percent of the world's population living in the south commands less than 12 percent of the gross world product.[75] Sivard has devised graphics detailing the distribution of world income, population, and unmet human needs. These graphics point out that the northern countries of North America, western and eastern Europe with high per capita incomes have correspondingly low percentages of infant mortality, adult illiterates, malnutrition, and people without safe water. But the southern countries of Latin America, Africa, the Middle East, and Oceania have just the reverse: a high percentage of infant deaths, adult illiterates, malnourished populations, and people without safe water.[76] She explains it as follows:

> Against the backdrop of income distribution, unmet social needs stand in strong contrast. Three of the poorest regions of the world, South Asia, the Far East (except Japan), and Africa have 19 percent of the world's economic product, but 83 percent of the infant deaths, 83 percent of people without adequate water supply, 88 percent of adult illiterates, 96 percent of the malnourished.[77]

Causes have effects. The actions of the world's highly developed industrialized societies cause reactions that reverberate throughout every nation of our "global village." The actions of our people—for good or for ill—have consequences for untold millions of our world neighbors. The following vignette illustrates the point.

> I asked the men, "What are you carrying in that hammock, brothers?" And they answered, "We are carrying a dead body, brother." So I asked . . . "Was he killed or did he die a natural death?" "This is difficult to answer, brother. It seems more to have been a murder." "How was the man killed? With a knife or bullet, brothers?" I asked. "It was neither knife or bullet; it was a much more perfect crime. One that leaves no sign." "Then how did they kill this man?" I asked, and they calmly answered: "This man was killed by hunger, brother."[78]

We are the killers; we, too, are the killed. We are the victimizers, and we are the victim. Through a myriad of causes, we are trapped in a murky mire, a pit from which there seems no escape, no exit, in Sartre's phrase. We thrash about; we offer meaningless assurances to ourselves and others: things will improve, won't they? If not this year, how about next? We blame somebody, anybody: the president, management, the union, the boss, the military, politicians, the technicians and scientists who created all this so-called progress in the first place. We blame God. We look for a hand to drag us out, a life ring to pull us to safety. But no hand is there. There is no one to throw the life rope because we are all sinking. We are all in the pit together. Where are you, Jesus? We are banging on the doors of heaven, yet we do not hear you answer us. God of Abraham, Isaac, and Jacob, Sarah, Rebecca, and Rachael: where are you? If not the God of the Israelites, if not Jesus, what about Allah, guardian of society: Where are you, Allah? And what about you, Mencius? Even before the Christian era, you transmitted the Confucian way and assured us that humankind is good. Where are you now, Mencius? Buddha, two and a half thousand years ago, you taught the people the meaning of universal loving-kindness. Where are your precepts now, Buddha? Gandhi, you are closer to us in time. You taught us, in the Hindu way, reverence for all of Creation and the meaning of the nonviolent quest for peace. Where are you now, great teacher? Great Spirit of the Sioux whose handiwork is in the sun, the moon, the trees, and the mountains: Where are you? We need you now, Great Spirit. Come quickly.

The Biblical motifs of creation, covenant and community provide funda-
mental perspectives and obligatory ideals which should inform our thoughts
and hopes. To stand before God as creator is to respect God's creation,
both the world of nature and that of human history

——Catholic Social Teaching and the
U.S. Economy

3. The Goodness of Creation: Biblical Motifs

In the Beginning

In the beginning is the Book of Genesis, the first of the five scrolls, the first of the five books of Moses that—taken together—comprise the basic arrangements of the life and progress of the founding of Israel's—and our—tradition. Genesis is the origin, the source.

In the beginning is Genesis—the account of humankind's beginnings and the setting out of the pattern of the universe; Exodus—the witness of God's action to deliver the people from slavery and bondage to bind them together with God and each other in covenant; Leviticus—a book of liturgy, laws, and guidance for God's people; Numbers—more laws, census, blessings, and instruction; and Deuteronomy—Moses' farewell, a restatement of the Law, and a rehearsal of the mighty acts of God. Taken together these five books are like a sweeping five-movement symphony, a symphony embracing a wide diversity of melodic and dissonant lines from the first note of time and being through Israel's pilgrimage as a people from Abraham to the Exile.

In the beginning, Genesis sets the tone for just and cordial relationships between people and toward the environment. Genesis describes a style of faithfulness human beings are expected to have toward God. Everett Fox, Hebrew scholar, has pointed out that "no major character in Genesis achieves success without depending fully on God, and the standards that are held up to them are ultimately seen as God's own, to be imitated by imperfect humankind."[1]

In the beginning, the Pentateuch (that is, the collection of the first five books we have been referring to) was the only part of the Bible recognized by all Jews as the authoritative foundation stone of the faith. It has thus been accorded a special place of importance in Hebrew tradition, just as the Gospels stand apart from the rest of the New Testament as central in Christian tradition.

In the beginning of the Pentateuch, Genesis itself stands out with an integrity of its own, for Genesis introduces the broad, sweeping themes of environment, of the nature of God and of humankind, of the order and meaning of history, of responsibility and covenant, of blessing, of evil and alienation, of temptation and struggle, sibling rivalry, testing, choice, and continuity. These fundamental themes presented in Genesis are motifs that reverberate throughout the entire Bible in both testaments. They are themes that have parallels in all religious and cultural traditions. Genesis is a study of contrasts and paired opposites: earth/heaven, darkness/light, perfection/reality, jealousy/harmony, transgression/retribution, discord/reconciliation, cause/effect, sterility/fertility, age/youth, blessing/curse.

The overwhelming simplicity and directness of Genesis' style, along with the awesomeness of its themes make this first chapter of the Bible a gem of poetic prose and one of the genuinely great pieces of world literature. Its haunting tones and its giant sweep of time and space and eternity presented in the measured tones of the sequence of days put us in touch with the roots of our own reality and the reality and destiny of every being and every phenomena of the natural world.

Since Genesis (and especially the first three chapters, which treat the Creation accounts) is basic to the development of both Jewish and Christian traditions, Genesis is the starting point for our appreciation of the Creation stories' wisdom. In a sense, we have to look backward in order that we might move forward with deeper understanding. In Claus Westermann's words,

> Reflection on the world as a whole occurs only in the reflection on creation on the overall history of early [humankind] . . . the world as a whole can only be understood in the context of its coming into being. Early man confronted the world of his time in its quite incomprehensible complexity and variety. The world was whole only through its coming into being as such; it was grasped as a totality in the reflection on creation.[2]

It is particularly important that we reclaim with fresh vitality the Creation narratives now and set them in our contemporary context, because they have been too readily dismissed as "mere myth" on the one hand and as heavy-handed, literal fundamentalism on the other, and in between they have been fraught with misunderstanding.

Reasons for the rape of Creation are often cited in the first chapter of Genesis, which reads,

> God said, "Let us make man in our image, after our likeness and let them *have dominion* over the fish of the sea and over the birds of the air, and over cattle, and over all the earth, and over every creeping thing that creeps upon the earth." So God created man in his own image, in the image of God he created them; male and female he created them. And God blessed them, and God said to them, "Be fruitful and multiply, and fill the earth and *subdue* it; and *have dominion* over the fish of the sea and over the birds of the air, and over every living thing that moves upon the earth." (Gen. 1:26–28)

The domination theme is echoed in Psalm 8:

> You give [humankind] *mastery over the works of your hands;* you put all things under his feet: all sheep and oxen, even wild beasts of the field, the birds of the air, the fish of the sea, and whatsoever walks in the paths of the sea. (Ps. 8:7–9)

Regrettably, the command to humankind to "have dominion" over the animals and to "subdue" the earth has been misinterpreted and misunderstood so as to suggest free license to exploit the natural world to selfish ends. This in turn has been exacerbated by church tradition that has had, at best, an ambiguous relationship with the world, at times in its long history even rejecting the material world altogether.

Let us, therefore, look at the Creation accounts to help us to understand.

Who am I? Where did I come from? How did it all begin at the beginning of time? These are identity questions; they are basic to all peoples, cultures, and religious traditions, and answers to them are all attempts to find our historical place in the cosmos. If I know where I have come from, I may learn who I am, where I—and my people—fit in, and where my people will be at a future time. Thus, it is not surprising that there are two Judeo-Christian accounts about our beginnings, the J (for Jahveh, Yahweh, Jehovah) and the P (for priestly) accounts.

Most scholars date the older account, the J (Gen. 2:4b–25) at about the ninth century B.C. It embodies the ancient Hebrew traditions from the Southern Kingdom of Judah and, like P, is probably the work of several authors. The P document, dating from the fifth century B.C., is the work of exiles returning from Babylon.

Neither of the accounts are to be taken literally, nor are they to be considered as the theoretical analysis of nature's beginnings. We cannot prove that they are correct from a scientific point of view. Rather they are to be taken, as Alan Richardson has suggested, as "masterpieces of poetic imagination."[3] The images in the Creation stories are also scattered liberally throughout both the Old and New Testaments: images of darkness and light, of heaven and earth and fertility, images of fruits and vegetables bringing forth their increase, images of relationships between God and God's Creation, images of goodness and plenty. In this respect Adam is universal man; Eve universal woman. To quote Richardson:

> . . . Adam, Eve, the Serpent, the Ark, and so on, are all poetical figures; they belong to the poetry of religious symbolism, not to history and geography. The truth with which they deal is not the literal truth of the actual observation of measurable things and events; it is ultimate truth which can be grasped only by the imagination, and which can be expressed only by image and symbolism.[4]

So it is not the literalness of the words, nor the sequence of the facts (which, in any case, differ in J and P). Rather, the Creation stories are most helpful when they are used as springboards to suggest a style of relationships between the members of God's Creation, human beings sharing their creatureliness with other animals yet also possessing higher consciousness and, therefore, higher responsibility. There is nothing to suggest that human beings are to dominate other people or that in ruling the natural world they are to rule *the forces of nature*. And the domination of animals ought to be interpreted as a loving, parental care, a co-care with God. Because it has also been acknowledged that all aspects of Creation—the animals and the plants, the seas and skies—are good, they are deserving of respect and loving consideration.

It takes both of the biblical Creation stories complementing each other to bring to light essential aspects of ourselves and our relationships to and in the natural world and to natural cycles. Let us touch on four themes illuminated in the Creation accounts, because they tell us something about ourselves and our relationship in the cosmos. These themes are earthiness, sabbath, blessing, and sin.

Earthiness:

In the J account, human beings are created from earth in the same manner as the animals.

> Then the Lord God formed man of dust from the ground, and breathed life into his nostrils, the breath of life; and man became a human being. (Gen. 2:7)

> And out of the ground the Lord God formed every beast of the field and every bird of the air. (Gen. 2:19)

That is, human beings and animals share the same beginnings; they have come from the same primal elements. It thus makes sense that aboriginal peoples typically understand the earth as mother—mother of humankind and animals. J highlights our common connectedness to the soil and thus to each other. According to Westermann, in reflecting on this relationship,

> the theological, psychological, and sociological aspects of this philosophy [of relationships] can be summed up in the one sentence: no one can be isolated from his fellow . . . that man is by nature, at the same time, just as much a creature as he is a member of community.[5]

We are reminded of the earthiness of our beginnings at every Ash Wednesday liturgy during the imposition of ashes when the presiding minister repeats these familiar words with every participant while rubbing ashes on their foreheads: "Almighty God, you have created us out of the dust of the earth. . . . Remember that you are dust, and to dust you shall return."

Although human beings are given a special place of responsibility in the natural world, they also share with other beings of God's created order a common beginning and a common destiny, a common cycle of life and death.

Our Jewish forebears have never forgotten their earthly beginnings, and their tradition has never lost sight of humankind's indebtedness to the earth. All of the three great pilgrim feasts in Jewish tradition are rites of thanksgiving for the Lord's natural abundance: Passover marks the early harvesting of the barley; Shavuot commemorates the harvesting of the wheat and the beginning of the fruit harvest; and Sukkot marks the final harvest of the year. Of the three, it is the Sukkot Festival (or the Feast of Booths) that most consciously makes the connection between humankind and the environment. It is planned to coincide with the culminating harvest of the year "after the ingathering from the threshing floor and the wine press." For its seven-day duration, Jewish families are enjoined to live outside in natural surroundings, in booths decorated with leafy boughs and fruits of the land. At harvest time, booths are built everywhere—on fire escapes in New York City, on the roofs of Tel Aviv apartment buildings, in backyards all over the world.

The Sukkot ritual consists of holding the branches of four plants to the winds in the direction of the four corners of the globe to fulfill the biblical injunction to "take some of the best fruit from your trees, your palm branches and limbs from leafy trees, and begin a religious festival to honor the Lord your God" (Lev. 23:40). Another Sukkot ritual utilizes water on which the harvest depends and in compliance with the command that "with joy you shall draw water out of the wells of salvation" (Isa. 12:3). In ancient times, Sukkot was regarded as the outstanding festival of the year, indicated by the fact that old talmudic sources often referred to it simply as "the Festival."[6]

Created by God out of God's earth, we share with all creatures of God's created order a common earthy destiny. Our travels throughout our lifetimes may take us to the furthest reaches of interplanetary space, yet earthlings we remain. And lest this be interpreted as mere pantheism, let us recall the words of that most endearing of saints, St. Francis, whose "Canticle of the Sun" is a song of praise for the joys of God's Creation and his (and our) relationships with all its aspects:

> Most high, all powerful, all good Lord!
> All praise is yours, all glory, all honor, and all blessing.
> To you alone, Most High, do they belong.
> No mortal lips are worthy to pronounce your name.
> All praise be yours, my Lord, through all you have made,
> And my first lord, Brother Sun,
> Who brings the day; and light you gave us through him.
> How beautiful is he, how radiant in all his splendor!
> Of you, Most High, he bears the likeness.
> All praise be yours, my Lord, through Sister Moon and Stars;
> In the heavens you have made them bright and precious and fair.
> All praise be yours, my Lord, through Brother Wind and Air,
> And fair and stormy, all the weather's moods,
> By which you cherish all that you have made,
> All praise be yours, my Lord, through Sister Water,
> So useful, lowly, precious and pure.
> All praise be yours, my Lord, through Brother Fire,
> Through whom you brighten up the night.
> How beautiful he is, how gay! Full of power and strength.
> All praise be yours, my Lord, through Sister Earth, our mother,
> Who feeds us in her sovereignty and produces various fruits and
>   colored flowers and herbs. . . .[7]

And Christians use the fruits of nature—wheat and grapes—which, through human interaction, become bread and wine of heaven and the central symbols of our rite of Holy Communion—holy community—with God and among each other and all Creation.

Sabbath:

The P account recounts that

> on the seventh day God finished the work which he had done, and he rested on the seventh day from all the work which he had done. So God blessed the seventh day and hallowed it, because on it God rested from all his work which he had done in creation. (Gen. 2:2–3)

God at work and God at rest; God in action, God in repose; God engaged, God at ease; God in effort, God in pause; God in creating,

God in stillness; God in the thunderclap, God in the silence and calm. In some respects the seventh day gives meaning to the other six, for in it we picture a resting God in Creation, a God who pauses to let the magnificence of the created order penetrate him. For six days God has worked on the natural world; now God stands aside to allow the natural world to affect him. "And God saw that it was good." It is a divine reciprocity, a divine rhythm: God acts in the first instance, and in the second God is acted upon.

The seventh day is a part of the unfolding of Creation. It is not apart from it. The seventh day gives meaning to the other six, for on it God stands aside—not outside—and in a posture of inactivity, he comprehends the meaning of his activity. Thus, it is not a thing—neither an animal nor a plant—that is hallowed with a blessing but *a time,* a segment of time that is hallowed not for itself but for the larger reality, for the other six days. In the hallowing of the seventh day, God looks back on the previous six, and he looks ahead to a pattern of living for God's people: six days of work, one day of rest.

Work and leisure, activity, and rest, form the natural rhythm of existence. So it is not surprising that P named the rest day and called it sabbath, for God's sabbath mimics the natural sabbath that would have been plainly evident, that *is* plainly evident. Children run about all day and sleep all night; felines sleep all day and roam all night—the rest afforded by sleep spurs the activity of wakefulness. Trees lay bare all winter long, and bulbs lie hidden in the soil only to burst into color and light with the first stirrings of spring warmth; fields lie fallow for a season only to grow with more energy in another season.

According to the Exodus account (Exod. 20:11 and 31:17), sabbath represents the rest God took on the seventh day of his Creation. And also in the Deuteronomy account, sabbath represents a time to remember the Israelites' deliverance out of the land of Egypt:

> You shall remember that you were a servant in the land of Egypt, and the Lord your God brought you out with a mighty hand and an outstretched arm; therefore the Lord your God commanded you to keep the sabbath day. (Deut. 5:15)

On the sabbath God rests; so also do all the other works of the Lord—"your ox, your ass, your cattle" (Deut. 5:14). All people are to rest, particularly those most burdened by their work—servants and laborers.

A Jewish source describes the meaning of sabbath this way:

> From of old the Jewish people have seen the sabbath as a unique gift, a token of their covenant with God. The sabbath is the most cherished creation of the Jewish spirit; it mirrors the essence of the Jewish soul.

. . . The sabbath is a symbol of triumph. In every age sabbath afforded the Jew a holy retreat, a haven of safety, a fountain of new strength and perpetual self-renewal. The sabbath nurtured family life in love and harmony; it united husband and wife, parent and child. . . . The sabbath is part of nature's design, the very purpose of creation; all that was created attained its consummation in the sabbath. This day is steeped in mystic splendor, a source of holiness; a symbol of the world's fulfillment.[8]

The very early Christians, after their conversion from Judiasm, kept the seventh day just as they had always done. In fact, the Seventh Day Adventists still keep the seventh day. But the timing—if not the concept of sabbath rest—began to change in the beginning of the Christian era. Since both Christ's resurrection and the coming of the Holy Spirit were said to have occurred on the first day of the week rather than the last, Sunday came to be set apart as a day also for the remembrance of Christ's resurrection (while at the same time retaining its earlier significance).

The sabbath was, in a certain sense, a time to set things right, a time even to readjust the order of society. Clearly related to the concept of sabbath is that of the sabbatical year, the one year in seven in which "there shall be a sabbath of solemn rest for the land, a sabbath to the Lord; you shall not sow your field or prune your vineyard" (Lev. 25:4). Out of the sabbath year arose the jubilee year—the year following the seven times seven (Lev. 25:8), the free fiftieth year in which the Jewish slaves were set free and land was returned to its former owners. It was a year of refreshment to readjust the balance sheet, to right former injustices, to usher in God's equality.

Molded after the natural rhythm of existence, patterned on God's sabbath of the seventh day—one day in seven; one year in seven; one year twice a century—the provision is made for God's creatures to rest. Sabbaths are interludes of restoration that give perspective to the wider canvas of reality, to the dominant activity of our lives: work. Josef Pieper went so far as to say even that sabbath is the basis of culture. In his book, *Leisure: The Basis of Culture*, he says,

We may read in Genesis that God "ended his work which he had made" and "behold it was very good." In leisure man too celebrates the end of his work by allowing his inner eye to dwell for a while upon the reality of the creation. He looks and he affirms: it is good. . . . It is a form of silence, of that silence which is the prerequisite of the apprehension of reality; only the silent hear and those who do not remain silent do not hear. . . . [It is] the soul's power to "answer" to the reality of the world.[9]

Blessing:

Closely related to the concept of sabbath is that of blessing. That is the pronouncement of God's favor. The locations of blessing in the P account are significant. In the first case (Gen. 1:22) God creates fish and fowl with the command that they "be fruitful and multiply." In the second instance (Gen. 1:28), God is pictured as blessing the people he has created, and he does so in connection with a command. "And God blessed them, and God said to them, 'Be fruitful and multiply, and fill the earth and subdue it.' " With God's blessing comes the command, "Be fruitful and multiply"; share the blessing, in other words. God's favor is not to be kept, not to be hoarded; God's favor is to be shared abundantly. God's blessing and humankind's action are indissoluably linked. In the confidence of God's blessing, humankind is charged to go forward into the future to perform its tasks of replenishing and subduing the earth. Significant also is the fact that God has not only given humankind the assurance of the divine blessing; God has also made provision for strength and nourishment to perform the tasks. "Behold, I have given you every plant yielding seed which is upon the face of the earth, everything that has the breath of life. I have given you every green plant for food" (Gen. 1:29).

In the third instance, after the six days of God's creative activity, God's blessing is used in relationship to sabbath. "So God blessed the seventh day and hallowed it" (Gen. 2:3a). The wonders, the riches, the unspeakable joys of Creation evoked from God two responses: sabbath rest and blessing; pause to comprehend and praise to give thanks. The response of God is blessing, and we are, therefore, obliged to live our lives in light of God's blessing.

Blessing is three dimensional. It is grounded in the soil of the present; it looks with gratitude to the past, to the historical remembrance of God's blessing in Creation; and it looks to future time.

It has been said that a conscientious Jew sees God's providence in every experience and therefore praises and gives God thanks continually.

> The benediction [blessing] is essentially an utterance of gratitude for God's beneficence, for the privilege of experiencing God's manifestations in nature, and for the privilege of performing the commandments of the Torah. Since God's manifestations are to be found everywhere at all times, the pious Jew recites numerous benedictions. Indeed it is the goal of the pious Jew to recite daily not less than one hundred benedictions.[10]

The purpose of such regular repeating of benedictions is to deepen the individual's awareness of God's beneficence and to bestow an aura of holiness on ordinary things and ordinary experiences of life.

> Thus eating bread [becomes] not only an occasion for worship but an act of consecration. Life as a whole [becomes] a religious adventure.[11]

The Jewish blessing begins with the focus on God—"Blessed are thou, O Lord, King of the Universe"—then shifts to the present or future situation. Everything is cause for blessing, and sometimes a blessing is a charge, such as God's charge to Abraham: "Go forth from the land of your kinsfolk and from your father's house to the land that I will show you. I will make you a great nation, and I will bless you" (Gen. 12:1–2).

At other times a blessing is a consolation. The suffering Job said, "Naked I came from my mother's womb, and naked shall I return; the Lord gave and the Lord has taken away; blessed be the name of the Lord" (Job 1:21). When my grandmother was married she started a family prayer book that is used whenever the family gathers for a wedding, baptism, or funeral. She carefully recorded the occasions of its use in the front of the book. It happened that I was leafing through its pages as I was riding to her funeral. As I did so, I was powerfully struck at the inscription she had made at the time of the death of her young son many years before. It was the same as Job's at his time of testing: "The Lord gave and the Lord has taken away; blessed be the name of the Lord."

As Jesus prepared for the feeding of the five thousand he offered a blessing: ". . . taking the five loaves and two fish he looked up to heaven, and blessed, and broke and gave the loaves to the disciples, and the disciples gave them to the crowd" (Matt. 14:19). Jesus' blessing has become the centerpiece for the Eucharistic Prayer (Prayer of Consecration) during which God's people gather together to receive God's blessing and then, strengthened by it, go out into the world and act out God's blessing in their families, in their communities, in their workplaces, and in the political and civic structures of society.

Blessing is the assurance of God's favor. Through blessing we recall God's mighty acts in Creation; through blessing we are nourished in the present time; and with God's blessing we look with assurance to Creation's future time. All kinds of blessing, from the invocation of God's blessing at the rising of the sun on the new day to the prayer of blessing on the lips of the dying at the threshold of death; all these are played out against the sweeping backdrop of all Creation praising the Lord.

Included in the Apocryphal literature of the Bible is the story of the Three Young Men, said to be Jewish captives in Babylon, who were about to be punished for their refusal to worship the golden image Nebuchadnezzar had set up. At the moment of their death in a fiery furnace they sang out their song, which is an exhortation to all living creatures and every aspect of Creation to praise the Lord, the Creator of all. The unknown hymn writer must have derived inspiration from the antiphonal liturgy in Psalm 148, for both the psalm and verses 35 through 68 of the Song of the Three Young Men present the notion of all of God's Creation blessing God the Creator. From its opening phrase, "Bless the Lord, all works of the Lord" (Song of the Three Young Men, vs. 35), we are presented with the compelling image of the sun, moon, stars, fire, water, seasons, the weather (even lightning and clouds), as well as all manner of plants, animals, and people, praising God. The Song of the Three Young Men is aptly called the Song of Creation; it is the most complete and comprehensive blessing to be found anywhere in biblical literature. And it can be said that the destiny of the world rests upon our capacity to live in the spirit of the Song of the Three Young Men in loving responsibility to God's Creation and to allow its ideal of goodness and wholeness to penetrate every aspect of our being as we allow its rhythm to carry God's Creation into God's future.

Sin:

This is the century during which more innocent victims have been killed then in every other century put together, and it is sin in its many guises that has been the killer behind the killer. Untold millions of innocents have been killed in German gas chambers; in Japanese cities and on Pacific atolls by radiation; on European battlefields, in Korea, Vietnam, and Angola, in Israel and in the Gaza Strip, in South African townships; in English villages and Russian towns by nuclear power plant accidents; in Latin American torture chambers. They have died the slow death by starvation on African deserts; they have died of exposure on park benches and in alleys between abandoned buildings in the great cities of North America because there was no room to be found at the inn. Sin is the silent killer of the Brazilian rain forests; sin, the killer of fish in Long Island Sound and in the Gulf of Mexico; sin is behind the rape of the land.

Yet this is the century that wants to know as little as possible about sin or, when it does, is more likely than not to consider sin in terms of individual transgression (i.e., what the pious Christian would visit the confessor about) rather than as the massive failure of public responsibility. And if there is anything worse than sin, it is our failure to acknowledge and recognize sin and its destructive power. Karl Menninger lamented the phenomena of our lack of consciousness about sin or, to be more specific, our rejection of the notion of sin, and he called his book dealing with the subject *Whatever Became of Sin?* But Matthew Fox, on the other hand, in *Original Blessing*, has accused the Western church, and particularly Augustine, of altogether too much stress on Original Sin. So severe and negative has the Western church's stress on sin been, according to Fox, that "original sin grew to become the starting point for Western religion's flight from nature, creation, and the God of creation."[12]

Historically, a great deal of ink has been spilled by the churches over the doctrine of Original Sin. And Fox's argument has some merit since most of the churches have not focused on the meaning of sin in such a way as to promote corrective action. This author, however, would not reject the concept of sin in favor of blessing, for, it seems to me, that *only* in the recognition of the power of sin does one gain the capacity to counter the effects of sin. And certainly the concept of blessing does not suffer with a rejection of sin. Actually, blessing is enhanced when it is held in tension with sin. The paired opposites of blessing and sin need to be held together in balance. This essentially is what the Hebrew prophets did.

The authors of the J narrative were wise to include sin as a part of the Creation narrative, for doing so is an acknowledgment of sin as an existential fact of the human condition, as the universal enemy within people and, by extension, within all societies and cultures.

The account of Adam and Eve in the garden is what Herman Gunkel has termed an "aetiological" story, that is, an account that is an explanation of some phenomena that cannot be backed up by facts or scientific data. J straightforwardly explains the actual human condition, the way things are, period. J offers neither theories nor reasons but simply states the facts. That the Creation stories are aetiology in no way detracts from the soundness of their precepts.

> Now the serpent was more subtle than any other creature that the Lord God had made. He said to the woman, "Did God say, 'You shall not eat of the fruit of the trees in the garden?' "
> And the woman said to the serpent, "We may eat of the fruit of the trees of the garden; but God said, 'You shall not eat of the fruit which is in the midst of the garden, neither shall you touch it lest you die.' "
> But the serpent said to the woman, "You will not die. For God knows that when you eat of it your eyes will be opened, and you will be like God, knowing good and evil."
> So when the woman saw that the tree was good food, and that it was a delight to the eyes, and that the tree was to be desired to make one wise, she took of its fruit and ate; she also gave some to her husband, and he ate.
> Then the eyes of both were opened, and they knew that they were naked; and they sewed fig leaves together and made themselves aprons.

> When they heard the sound of the Lord God, moving in the garden in the cool of the day, the man and his wife hid themselves from the presence of the Lord God among the trees of the garden. But the Lord God called to the man, and said to him, "Where are you?" And he said, "I heard the sound of you in the garden, and I was afraid, because I was naked; and I hid myself." He said, "Who told you you were naked? Have you eaten of the tree which I commanded you not to eat?"
>
> The man said, "The woman you gave to me, she gave me of the fruit and I ate." Then the Lord God said to the woman, "What is this that you have done?" The woman said, "The serpent beguiled me and I ate." (Gen. 3:1–13)

Taken together, these few verses summarize what we know to be true of sin:

1. However inexplicable it may seem, sin is a part of the basic design of the universe. The serpent, after all, was created by God (Gen. 3:1). And furthermore sin is tied to the destructive instinct that slumbers within all of us.

2. Sin is subtle (Gen. 3:1) and often difficult to identify.

3. Sin leads to idolotry, to the setting up of oneself or someone or something else to be like God or to take the place of God. The serpent said, ". . . you will be like God, knowing good and evil" (Gen. 3:5). Eating of the tree confers the power to be like God. Alan Richardson has suggested that this knowing is not the academic way of having knowledge but rather knowing in the Hebrew sense of implying knowledge that comes from practical experience. What is implied is that humankind attempts to be like God, determining for itself what is good or evil, rather than relying on God to determine right from wrong. According to Richardson, this desire on the part of humankind to be like God "is the fatal weakness of human nature: man's [and woman's] desire to give glory to himself [and herself] and not to the Creator, to usurp the place of God and put him [her] self up in the position which belongs to God alone."[13]

4. However much people have—whether it be opportunity or material goods—part of the human condition is that we desire most what we do not have or what is forbidden (Gen. 2:16–17). The teenager has a whole refrigerator full of soft drinks at his or her disposal but prefers the contents of the parents' liquor cabinet. Or, an ordinary house was more than adequate until the homeowner saw his neighbor's with deck, swimming pool, and Jacuzzi. Or, our country has an arsenal large enough to blow up the earth many times over but wants a Star Wars system it does not have.

5. Sin leads to hiding, to cover up (Gen. 3:7). Until Adam and Eve ate the apple, they did not know they were naked. Without sin, Adam and Eve had nothing to hide from each other, nor did they

need to hide from God (Gen. 3:8). There would be no reason for the C.I.A. to conduct covert activities unless they had something to hide. The Watergate and Iran-Contra investigations were as much examinations of attempts to cover up the facts as they were exposures into what crimes actually occurred. Sin leads to cover up.

6. With sin comes blame, that is, the failure to take responsibility for sin. In the first instance, Adam blamed Eve (Gen. 3:12), and in the second, Eve blamed the serpent (Gen. 3:13). The accident was someone else's fault. Homelessness has become a way of life for many during the Reagan era because of the policies of the Reagan administration (rather than because of my failure to use my power to influence public policy). Sin carries blame in its wake.

A prominent theorist of the Social Gospel, Walter Rauschenbusch, said,

> Human nature is quick to seize the chance [to unload responsibility for sin]. Man [and woman] unloaded on original sin, on the devil, and on the decrees of God. Adam began soon after the fall to shift the blame. This shiftiness seems to be one of the clearest and most universal effects of original sin.[14]

7. Sin leads to alienation between people and between people and God. "I am putting enmity between you and the woman" (Gen. 3:15). And the greater the sin, the more profound will be the alienation that follows, so that in the final case human beings are alienated from each other, from God, and from the environment. According to the Catholic bishops pastoral on the U.S. economy,

> . . . the sin of our first parents had consequences. . . . Alienation from God pits brother against brother (Gen. 4:9) in a cycle of war and vengeance. Sin and evil abound, and the primeval history culminates in another assault on the heavens, this time ending in a battle of tongues scattered over the face of the earth (Gen. 11:1–9). Sin simultaneously alienates human beings from God and shatters the solidarity of the human community.[15]

But lest we lose heart, let us remember that sin can also be a great teacher, for as William James said in an earlier age, "*evil facts . . . are a genuine portion of reality; and they may, after all be the best key to life's significance, and possibly the only openers of our eyes to the deepest levels of truth.*" [emphasis added].[16]

Continuing Creation

The natural motifs of earthiness, sabbath, blessing, and sin are played out throughout the entire Bible. Blessing and sin motifs especially, in all their manifold variations, occupy center stage against which the earthiness and sabbath motifs form the backdrop.

Human beings' failure to accord Yahweh centrality in their personal lives and in society and to conduct themselves accordingly has been offered as the explanation for famine and destruction, and the prophetic literature is repleat with warnings that the forces of nature would turn against human communities if they continued sinning.

Start with the Cain and Abel story, for instance. Cain has killed his brother Abel. Therefore, he is told, "When you till the ground, it shall no longer yield to you its strength; you shall be a fugitive and a wanderer on the earth" (Gen. 4:12). So Cain, who had taken matters into his own hands and murdered Abel, is to be punished by an inhospitable land and alienation from it. There is Moses' warning. The people will indeed be blessed with prosperity in the land but with a condition: "Never forget the Lord your God or turn to other gods to worship and serve them. If you do, then I warn you today that you will certainly be destroyed" (Deut. 8:19). The prophet Jeremiah, in criticizing the people for their worship of other gods, announces that "because you have forsaken me and served foreign gods in your land, so you shall serve strangers in a land that is not yours" (Jer. 5:19b). For a society that is given to idol worship and lack of respect among people, Ezekiel gives the Lord's warning: "I will make the land a desolation and a waste" (Ezek. 33:28a).

The prophet is so fused and identified with God that he speaks as if his voice were that of God. The prophet speaks words of rebuke, not for punishment's sake, but in order to reestablish God's sovereignty, so "then you will know that I am the Lord" (Ezek. 33:29).

> Love motivates the prophet and he speaks words of rebuke *because* he loves the people, for as we can see, the sharpest rebukers of the prophets—Hosea and Jeremiah—are also the most ardent in their love for the people.[17]

Seeds of the linear nature of God's time and the progression toward God's "new Creation" appear in Second Isaiah as the prophet looks forward to

> new heavens and a new earth. . . . I will rejoice in Jerusalem, and be glad in my people; no longer shall be heard in it the sound of weeping and the cry of distress. No longer shall there be in it an infant that lives but a few days, or an old man that does not fill out his days, for the child shall die a hundred years old. . . . They shall build houses and inhabit them; they shall plant vineyards and eat their fruit. They shall not build and another inhabit; they shall not plant and another eat; for like the days of a tree shall the days of my people be, and my chosen shall long enjoy the work of their hands. They shall not labor in vain, or bear children for calamity; for they shall be the offspring of the blessed of the Lord, and their children with them. Before they call I will answer, while they are yet speaking I will hear. The wolf and the lamb

shall feed together, and the lion shall eat straw like the ox. . . . They shall not hurt or destroy in all my holy mountain, says the Lord. (Isa. 65:17–25)

This theme of perfection harks back to the wholesomeness and simplicity of the Genesis Creation accounts. It is an image of a new heaven and a new earth in which all Creation will be united, renewed, refreshed, and transformed. How appropriate then that it finds its final restatement in the culminating chapters of the New Testament in which John has a vision of the New Jerusalem: "Then I saw a new heaven and a new earth . . ." (Rev. 21:1a).

Jesus and Paul: Continuing Creation in Jewish Tradition

The Fourth Gospel gives us a glimpse into the unity of the universe. In it, John takes us behind the scenes of Jesus' earthly ministry to set him in the context of all time and eternity. And however difficult it may be to comprehend, Jesus in the Johannine version was "in the beginning with God; [and] all things were made through him, and without him was not anything made that was made" (John 1:2–3).

Jesus, a Jew, was raised in Jewish scriptural tradition. His mission was the recovery and fulfillment of universal Jewish vocation; thus, he never departed from his Semitic roots. All of the Old Testament literature of which we have spoken in this chapter is Jesus' heritage (and ours). So although Jesus said very little about the care of God's physical Creation, we can assume that he did not have to since, as a devout Jew, he would have taken for granted the traditional attitudes of his people. (This is not to say that he did not criticize the tradition—like the rebuke to those who would put sabbath ritual before the needs of the people.)

We know that Jesus lived his life close to the natural world because his teachings are full of images taken from the environment: "Look at the birds in the air . . ." (Matt. 6:26a); "Consider the lilies of the field . . ." (Matt. 6:28). And he used natural symbols of daily life to illustrate the truths of his parables: seeds—the parable of the sower; yeast—the parable of yeast; the mustard seed; salt; the parable of the lost sheep. Jesus used the symbols of trees and vines: the parable of the vineyard, the lesson of the fig tree. Ordinary loaves and fishes were symbols of feeding.

Jesus was about universal salvation, and the destinies of people were the focus of that mission. As such, he relied upon people to work toward that universal salvation and fulfillment of all Creation. So if Jesus concentrated on people, this is not to suggest that he rejected the material world. Rather, from all his references to it, we can infer that *he assumed it.*

Jesus is not only the fulfillment of the old Jewish covenant; Jesus is the sign of God's new covenant with the people. Here God is so much identified with the people of God's Creation that God became a human being in Jesus, a human being whose very blood, poured out for the people of God's Creation, creates a new covenant and a new people. The earthiness of the old covenant and the humanity of the new is perfectly summarized in the Mark account of Jesus' last supper with his disciples: "And he said to them, 'This is my blood of the covenant which is poured out for many. Truly I say to you, I shall not drink again of the vine until the day when I drink it new in the Kingdom of God' " (Mark 14:24–25). Vine—the earthiness of the old covenant. Jesus—the person of the new.

The theme of Christian faith as continuity and fulfillment of Jewish religion is carried on in the Acts of the Apostles. Throughout, the intimate link between the people of God and Creation is always assumed. Paul and Barnabas charged the people not to be led astray or turn to false gods but to be faithful "to the living God who made heaven, earth, sea, and all that is in them" (Acts 14:15b) and assured them of God's dependability. "He has always given evidence of his existence by the good things he does: he gives us rains from heaven and fruitful seasons . . ." (Acts 14:17b).

Paul's stress is on God in the saving person of Jesus Christ, in whom all aspects of Creation are incorporated and summarized, and that "if anyone is in Christ, he is a new creation, the old has passed away, behold, the new one has come" (2 Cor. 5:17). Consequently, it has been said that Paul is no friend of Creation and that ecologists and environmentalists would do well to pay him little heed. Furthermore, Paul is frequently being interpreted as—in effect—giving permission to Christians to turn away from the natural world and to concentrate on the life of the spirit.

But perhaps Paul has been done a disservice, for while it is true that his focus is the saving power of Christ, the development of lives of faith, and the establishment of Christian communities, Paul, like Jesus, was a Jew steeped in Jewish scriptural tradition with its inherent ethos of the intrinsic worth of every aspect of the created order. "Ever since the creation of the world God's invisible nature, namely his eternal power and diety, has been clearly perceived in the things that have been made" (Rom. 1:20). Also it was the *sins* of the world and the flesh (Romans 1 and 8) that Paul warned against, not the world as such. Paul, like the writer of the Fourth Gospel, places Jesus at the beginning of time, at the heart of the unfolding drama of Creation, and he saw his own ministry as that of preaching "the unsearchable riches of Christ and to make everyone see what is the plan of the mystery hidden for ages in God who created all things" (Eph. 3:9).

The Framework for God's Future

The God who acted at the center of the Creation of the world continues to act in the seasons and rhythms of life: in the fresh spring and in the abundant harvest, in peoples and prophets and in human communities that have called and continue to call humankind back from the brink of sin and idolatry, that continue to act in the world as God's co-creators. According to Kim Yong-Bock of the Presbyterian Theological Seminary in Seoul, Korea,

> In this new Covenant [in Galations 3, 4, and 5] community there is no order that separates the poor from the rich, the slave from the master, the foolish from the wise, the powerless from the powerful, or the Gentiles from the Jews. . . . The socio-economic security of the people of God is closely related to the integrity of the land, the earth and all the living creatures. Therefore it is natural to read and understand that God's Covenant with his people is inclusive of the earth as the integral covenant partner.[18]

At times the Creation motifs of our earthiness, of sabbath, of blessing, and sin have seemed remote and distant from us, and unable to grasp the simplicity of their wisdom, we have made light of our obligation to God who both loves his created world unconditionally but also requires our unconditional response to care for Creation. The critical nature of our present age makes it absolutely imperative that Christians develop a Creation-centered theology and spirituality, but let us admit the serious problems we encounter in attempting to do so. The Episcopal Church's Standing Commission on Peace summarizes the problem:

> Unlike Taoism, or the buoyant Judaism of Deuteronomy 8:7–8, or the creation-oriented spirituality of some Native American religions, Christianity has not traditionally sprung to mind as a principal source for a theology of the environment. To be sure, the doctrine of the Incarnation (nature as the host of the divine), with its attendant premise that the linking of body and spirit is no liability, and that of the Resurrection (that matter can partake of the conditions of salvation) would appear to have guaranteed a more central place for the environment in Christian theology. In fact the opposite has been the case.[19]

The Christian encounters problems of both biblical fact and biblical interpretation. From Creation to new Creation, Christianity moves in a linear sequence toward a conclusion of history. References to Christ's Second Coming and to an end time are scattered throughout the Gospels and the rest of the New Testament. For example: "Just as the weeds are gathered up and burned in the fire, so the same thing will happen *at the end of time*" (Matt. 13:40); "And this Good News about the Kingdom will be preached through all the world for a witness to everyone, and then the *end will come*"

(Matt. 24:14); *"The end of all things is near"* (1 Pet. 4:7); also see 1 Cor. 1:18; and the final chapters of the Revelation of John, which refer to a new heaven and a new earth, the new Jerusalem and Jesus' Second Coming (Revelation 21 and 22).

That Jesus' Second Coming and the Apocalypse were expected by our early church forebears has been a continuing problem for Christians and so have the interpretations—most of them deficient—which have exacerbated the issue: that Creation was a static, once-only event rather than a continuous unfolding and carrying out of God's creativity; that since the natural world is "fallen" and corrupted anyway, we can let it go because the old Creation will be rescued by the new Creation and Christ's Second Coming. We will be given the opportunity to bail out, as it were, and given a second chance. But deficient as these and other interpretations may be, they are widely held and highly influencial. For example, when James Watt, former Secretary of the Interior in the early days of the Reagan administration, was criticized for issuing what many environmentalists considered an inordinate number of permits for mineral exploration in federal forest lands over which he had jurisdiction, he made light of the matter. He did so because, as he was fond of saying, the end time was near so why worry since all Creation is ultimately going to end in destruction anyway. Watt's apocalyptic thoughts are both widespread and dangerous.

Attitudes such as Watt's, and other similarly faulty interpretations of the faith, as well as the apocalyptic Scripture of our tradition, have left Christians wide open to criticism by ecologists, environmentalists, and adherents of native religions. Vine Deloria, Jr., a Lakota Indian and author of *God Is Red*, for example, blames Christians for their "shallow understanding of ecological destruction" and contends that it is Christians' "religious attitude that has largely been responsible for the crisis."[20]

Deloria's criticism notwithstanding, the overall weight of the Bible does indeed suggest an ethic of responsibility regarding the natural world, but all the same we cannot afford to be blind to our problems or the limitations of our tradition.

However much we may attempt to limit God's activity, to, in Bonhoeffer's terms, accept "cheap grace," the Creation motifs stand as ideals to challenge and to inform our thought and provide the framework for humankind's present and future. These ancient, yet contemporary biblical themes remind us that, to quote the Catholic bishops' pastoral,

> to stand before God as creator is to respect God's creation, both the world of nature and that of human history. Misuse of the resources of the world or appropriation of them by a minority of the world's population

betrays the gift of creation meant for all people who are created in God's image with the mandate to make the earth fruitful. Creation by God and recreation by Christ make us realize that the communality we share with people of other nations is more basic than the barriers national borders create. A true Biblical vision of the human condition relativizes the claim of any state or government to total allegiance. It also makes us realize that people of other nations and with other ways of living share equally in God's image and should be equal recipients of God's bounty.[21]

The human being was made to breathe the good air of nature, but what he breathes is an obscure compound of acids and coal tars. He was created for a living environment, but he dwells in a lunar world of stone, cement, asphalt, glass, iron and steel. The trees wilt and blanch among sterile stone facades. Cats and dogs disappear little by little from the city, going the way of the horse. Only rats and men remain to populate a dead world.

——Jacques Ellul

4. Turning from Creation

Shaking of the Foundations

In truth, humankind probably began the long retreat from dependence upon the natural world the first day ancient people in northern climes built fireplaces inside their caves and blocked the openings to keep out the drafts.

And lest anyone bewail the benefits of "progress," just take a walk through any colonial graveyard of New England and note the grave markers of young mothers who died in their late teens or early twenties while giving birth, or the stones of infants who didn't make it to two. And who of us would tolerate being tied in the dentist's chair, like our grandparents, to have a tooth extracted? And one need only spend a couple of weeks on a remote Pacific atoll to appreciate the benefits of electricity, plumbing, and refrigeration. So the following pages neither suggest a rejection of progress nor are they a romantic longing for the days when Creation was in its pristine state. Rather they are merely a statement of circumstances and events that have contributed to our loss of dependence on the natural world, our altered perceptions of ourselves in relationship to God as author of Creation, and finally the gradual undermining of the church's understanding of Creation and humankind's place in the created order.

Ever since the proverbial human being brought a fireplace into the cave and closed the door to the elements, races and cultures and nations have moved from wandering tribal modes of living to settled agrarian centers and towns. They have tilled the land and lived off its riches; they have fished the seas and rivers and eaten of its gifts. Indeed, throughout our long journey as a people, human creativity has continued the work of Creation. If this were not so, if the whole act of Creation was completed in a week, humankind would not have survived, for our forebears would have died of boredom. Although farms and towns and even cities became more defined and dwellings more elaborate with the passage of time, Christians' belief in God the Creator and their acknowledgment of the truth of the Creation accounts remained unaltered until roughly the fifteenth century.

But through the march of time in its journey through the ages there developed a gap between belief in biblical tradition and the realities of society and human progress. That gap between church and society was ultimately to become the gaping chasm it is today. By the time the Augustinian monk Martin Luther nailed the Ninety-five Theses to the door of Castle Church in Wittenberg on the eve of All Saints' Day in 1517—thus beginning the Protestant Reformation—he was already acting out of a milieu increasingly uncomfortable with the church's view of the world that was becoming steadily irreconcilable with what was happening in the rest of society.

Churches had become static institutions, heavy under the burden of clericalization and corruption.[1] They were losing their hold as centers of culture, community, and authority. And while the church was losing ground and its authority questioned, there was a parallel explosion of secular learning and the development of a self-consciously secular spirit. Universities were built apart from the watchful eye of Mother Church. The age saw the flowering of painting, sculpture, architecture, and music. Brunelleschi, Donatello, Michelangelo, Leonardo da Vinci, Raphael, Titian, Holbein, and Breughel introduced new dimensions of shape and vitality as artists began to look at the world of the present in new ways apart from the church.

And just as artists' perceptions of beauty and shape found expression in the secular world, a flood of explorations and discoveries changed peoples' thinking about their physical environment. Amerigo Vespucci, the Cabots, Cortez, Vasco de Gama, Magellan, and Christopher Columbus widened the boundaries of humankind's physical surroundings and possibilities. If Columbus believed that he could reach the East by sailing west then perhaps the world was not so vast as hitherto believed. Never mind that Columbus never made it to the East himself, that the possibility was conceivable was breakthrough enough.

And as explorers widened geographical horizons, the astronomer, Nicolaus Copernicus, narrowed them. In 1543 he broke with long tradition supported by both scientists and theologians and made the revoluntionary discovery that the earth revolves around the sun and not the reverse. Since earth could no longer be understood as the center, such knowledge began to change peoples' fundamental orientation in the universe. As I have written in *The Liberation of the Laity,*

> knowledge, imagination, creativity, color, artistry, light, expansion and alteration in understanding the physical universe—these were among the gifts of the Renaissance, indications that old ways were being transformed by the new. The foundations of the old world were crumbling; they could no longer hold the emergent civilization.[2]

Although the church survived this period of secular explosion, it survived as a divided church and one more concerned with the salvation of people than the salvation of the world. On this point, Moltmann has said,

> After its retreat from cosmology, theology concentrated on personal faith. "I believe, that God created *me* . . . ," as Luther's Short Catechism says. Of course all belief in creation includes that personal conviction. But this personal confession was now increasingly interpreted in an exclusive sense.[3]

Surely the foundations had begun to shake, and they would continue to do so, not so much due to any particular actions of the church (although Christendom in its divided state would no longer speak with one voice) but because of developments in the larger society that the churches simply could neither shape nor accommodate theologically.

The Scientific Revolution

Amid a church divided, the flourishing of secular art and architecture, and a new self-confidence in human possibility, scientific developments began to shed light on the nature of the world and of humanity. It was a revolution that began in the sixteenth century and reached its peak in the seventeenth. It was a revolution that began with Copernicus.

Inventors expanded the range of the universe. By the use of ordinary lenses, the range of reality now extended from a single cell to the most remote star. At one end of the spectrum, the telescope opened up the heavens and increased humankind's length vision. At the other end, the microscope enlarged humanity's immediate surroundings.

The Dutch mathematician Christian Huygens developed a mechanical clock, thus bringing the measurement of time from the sun and moon down to a simple machine. Lewis Mumford and

Jacques Ellul have both cited the clock as the single most important mechanical development of our culture. With the clock, according to Ellul,

> time was an abstract measure separated from the traditional rhythms of life and nature. It became mere quantity. From then on [after the invention of the clock] life itself was measured by the machine; its organic functions obeyed the mechanical. Eating, working, and sleeping were at the beck and call of machinery.[4]

The philosophical justification for the scientific revolution was expressed in the writings of Francis Bacon and René Descartes who held that the universe is a mechanical system that can be described in mathematical terms.

Isaac Newton, still considered by some the greatest scientist ever to have lived, described the principle of universal gravitation and the laws of motion. He provided an explanation for the fact that objects fall toward the earth as well as the rationale for the movement of heavenly bodies through the atmosphere. Bacon and John Locke and, somewhat later, Denis Diderot and Voltaire fostered belief in natural law and universal order and, above all, a confidence in human reason. Their rational and scientific approach to religion as well as to social and economic issues promoted a general sense of human progress and perfectibility—a view of the world unencumbered by the church. With their supreme faith in rational humanity established, they encouraged the discovery of universally valid principles that govern humanity, nature, and society. Their activity served as an implicit attack on the authority of the church.

The works of these men were widely disseminated, and their ideas were the focus of the intellectual elite in salons and drawing rooms throughout Europe. It is not that these philosophers and essayists of the age of the Scientific Revolution attacked the church as such (although some did), it is rather that the church was not a partner in the dialogue. There was the biblical account of how the world was created and the belief in the creativity of the universal God, on the one hand, and there were scientific explanations as to the nature of humanity and the workings of the universe, on the other. These opposing viewpoints were like two strangers passing in the night, going their separate ways, neither meeting in the darkness nor caring about the destination of the other. There was, according to Westermann, "no serious concern to build a bridge between the scientific explanations of the world and the biblical account of creation."[5]

The Industrial Revolution and on into the Twentieth Century

The explosion of knowledge, of art, architecture, beauty, and color; the expeditions and explorations of the Renaissance period; the scientific and mechanical inventions of the Scientific Revolution; and, above all, the self-confidence in human reason and human potential created a readiness and an expectation for rapid social change and the drastically altered life-styles of the masses of regular folk who would be affected by the Industrial Revolution. This period of transition from an agricultural society to a modern, industrial one is focused in England and can be roughly dated from 1750 to 1850. It is a century of major shifts in just about every aspect of life. Dramatic changes in social and economic structures took place, while inventions and technological innovations created the factory system, large-scale machine production, and greater specialization.

Prior to the Industrial Revolution, wood was the only fuel, and water, wind, and animal exertion the sole sources of power. But as the age progressed, wood was replaced by coal (which came along with the whole mining industry developed to wrest the coal from the ground), and a Scotsman, James Watt, perfected the steam engine (1769) and, incidentally, gave us the term *horsepower*.

The inventions of the fly shuttle, the spinning jenny, the frame and power loom made possible the modern textile industry. Coal mines of northern England coupled with textile factories to make Lancashire and Yorkshire the greatest textile centers in the world. And as factories sprang up, so roads were built for access and the transport of manufactured goods. Steamships and railroads were also developed.

Nor was the industrial activity confined to Britain. In America, Eli Whitney, a Yale graduate and mechanical genius, invented the cotton gin in 1793. It was a device for the rapid separation of seed from the cotton plant. And five years later Whitney developed standardized, interchangeable parts for the mass manufacture of muskets he produced in his New Haven factory. It was a development that would improve all factories everywhere, for now it was possible to manufacture all kinds of machines on a large scale.

As the century of the Industrial Revolution drew to a close, the manufacturing leaders of the age looked back over their harvest of coal, steam, and steel, of electricity and the gasoline engine, of new plants and factories and life-styles that had markedly altered people's perceptions of home and stability, of family, work, and money. And the changes were destined to continue. Taking advantage of the constant flow of inventions and developments, various modes of transportation continued to evolve and continued to make changes in the lives of people. These fitted in well with the westward expansion of the American people. In the United States, the East Coast was connected by train to the Great Lakes in 1850 and with Chicago in 1853. On the historic day of May 10, 1869, the Union Pacific and the Central Pacific railroads were joined together at Promontory Point, Utah, thus connecting the whole country "from sea to shining sea."

Not to be outdone by the railroad, two German engineers, Karl Benz and Gottlieb Daimler, built in the 1880s the first combustion engines. And on American shores, one Henry Ford, who had shown remarkable mechanical ability at an early age, left his father's farm in Dearborn to become an apprentice in a Detroit machine shop. With Horatio Alger's brand of pluck and luck, Ford's mechanical abilities plus his business canniness helped him to outdistance Ransom Olds, the Dodge brothers, and the Stanley brothers to become the reigning lord of the mass-produced automobile. In so doing, Ford put Detroit on the map as car capital of the world.

A major product of the Industrial Revolution, if it may be so expressed, was neither a manufactured object nor a mechanical innovation but a way of looking at and quantifying all that is created by human endeavor, namely, capitalism—that is, simply put, private ownership of the profits and the means of production. It is a system characterized by the concept of individual initiative and survival of the fittest. Capitalism is driven by the profit motive, and as it developed into the twentieth century, it called into being the vast network of banking, credit, advertising, and distribution institutions.

Oddly, though understandably, the British naturalist Charles Darwin became an apologist for the Industrial Revolution. Although finches, sea turtles, and giant iguanas may seem a far cry from the new age factory and its labor practices, his ideas about the survival in the natural world found application as justification for the emerging industrial system. And we can see how the jump from animals to people was made. Darwin reasoned that life is a constant competitive struggle in which some members possessed certain favorable traits. These traits were passed down from generation to generation through what he called a system of "natural selection" through which the fittest survive and, in so doing, the species is strengthened. Species able to adapt to present circumstances survive and flourish; those that are weak or maladaptive perish. In finding the key to unlock the mysteries of nature, Darwin, unwittingly perhaps, also found the means to justify a system many were finding questionable. According to Jeremy Rifkin,

> Darwin's theory succeeded precisely because it fit so well the tempers of the times. People readily identified with Darwin's view of how nature was organized because its basic tenets conformed so nicely with the way society was organizing itself and its own immediate environment. Darwin constructed a theory of nature that, in every particular, reinforced

the operating assumptions of the industrial order. In so doing he provided something much more valuable than a theory of nature. Darwin gave industrial man and woman the assurance they needed to prevail against any nagging doubts they might have regarding the correctness of their behavior. His theory confirmed what they so anxiously wanted to believe: that the way they were organizing their existence was indeed "harmonious" with the natural order of things.

Darwin's cosmology sanctioned an entire age of history. Convinced that their own behavior was in concert with the workings of nature, industrial man and woman were armed with the ultimate justification they needed to continue their relentless exploitation of the environment and their fellow human beings without even having to stop for a moment to reflect on the consequences of their actions.[6]

How odd it is that capitalism's severest critics, Marx and Engels, admired Darwin. Darwin fit their purposes, for they translated Darwinian ideas into their own theories of class struggle. Furthermore, these very different men can together be credited with making weighty contributions to the undermining of the historic place of the Creation accounts. In the "Manifesto of the Communist Party," for example, Marx and Engels acknowledge the demise of Christian ideas:

> [When the Industrial Revolution commenced] Christian ideas succumbed in the 18th century to rationalist ideas, feudal society fought its death battle with the then revolutionary bourgeoise. The ideas of religious liberty and freedom of conscience merely gave expression to the way of free competition within the domain of knowledge.[7]

And Engels continued the assault on the ancient biblical understanding of Creation:

> Nature is the proof of dialectics, and it must be said for modern science that it has furnished this proof with very rich materials increasing daily, and thus has shown that nature works dialectically and not metaphysically; that she does not move in the eternal oneness of a perpetually recurring circle, but goes through a real historical evolution. In this connection Darwin must be named before all others. He dealt the metaphysical conception of nature the heaviest blow by his proof that all organic beings, plants, animals and man himself, are the products of evolution going through millions of years.[8]

Imperceptably, a subtle drift was occurring in consciousness. Nature and the natural environment were coming to be seen as objects, things to be worked on, experimented with, manipulated, and exploited. As far as nature was concerned, it was not a matter of whether the system was capitalist or Marxist for, according to Moltmann,

> the destruction of the environment by the socialist industrial states does not fall behind the environmental destruction of the capitalist industrial

countries. Towards the different political systems, the ecological crisis is apparently neutral. Whether nature is destroyed by capitalist expansion or by socialist increased productivity makes no difference to nature. For the victim, nature, scientific and technological civilization is undoubtedly the most terrible monster ever to appear on earth.[9]

And let us not forget that it was not only nature in terms of the physical universe that had become a thing to be worked on—but human nature as well. If the world could be dissected, studied, experimented with, so could the human body. Medicine had taken a giant step into the modern world in the nineteenth century, which saw the beginnings of disinfection, innoculations, and anesthetics. It follows that if the human body could be safely dissected, why not the human mind as well? Enter Sigmund Freud, founder of psychiatry. As a young medical student in Vienna, Freud first began to develop his ideas by dissecting corpses from the city morgue. Moving from corpses to hysterical women, Freud would ultimately develop what might be called the architecture of the human mind. Whether or not Freud was correct in his theories and irregardless of developments by other early psychiatrists and psychoanalysts is not the point; what we have in Freud is a new way of examining human consciousness, emotions, and drives. Like everything else in the natural world, the human mind had also become object.

Perhaps the acknowledgment that religion had no place in the modern industrial world was a preferable stance than that of the apologists of capitalism who would imbue capitalism with religious significance. Andrew Carnegie, for example, was the personification of American capitalism. This head of the largest corporation the world had ever known, U.S. Steel, had in 1900 a personal income of $23 million with no income tax to pay.[10] When Carnegie, satisfied with his financial prowess, equated the Sermon on the Mount with what he called the "gospel of work," he articulated "the gospel of wealth."[11] Is it surprising then that the influential German sociologist, Max Weber, would associate the aescetism of Calvinism (erroneously, according to Lewis Mumford)[12] with the rise of capitalism? Weber's ideas, comforting to those like Carnegie who were profiting from capitalism, were published in his book *The Protestant Work Ethic and the Spirit of Capitalism*. With its publication we have a persuasive treatise on the uses of religion in support of an economic system.

With Christianity considered irrelevant to Marxists, on the one hand, and a tool to support capitalism, on the other, the churches were squeezed into either a defensive posture or coaxed into being the handmaids of industry and progress. Obviously, Christians' belief in the Creation stories, and particularly in the ethos of relationships between people and the environment that they suggest, was built on foundations long since shattered. They were regarded as beliefs only the most fundamentalist denominations could take with any degree of seriousness. The consequence, in Westermann's opinion, is that "the Church took only a defensive stand against the scientific explanation of the world and of man and had no renewed, vital presentation of the biblical reflection on the creator-creation to set against it."[13]

The churches' accommodation to a society that handsomely rewarded some and failed to challenge the "gospel of wealth" while tolerating the reality of others who were relegated to crowded, filthy, vermin-infested slums and factory towns did not go altogether unchallenged. The theologians and clergy of the Social Gospel were vocal in their repudiation of both unjust social practices and churches that went along with them. Walter Rauschenbusch, for example, spoke of the problem by describing the teachings of two of his colleagues:

> An eminent minister in New York ennumerated as the chief marks of a Christian that he attends church, reads the Bible, and contributes to the support of public worship. A less eminent minister in the same place mentioned as the four sins which a Christian must abstain: drinking, dancing, card playing, and going to the movies. And this in New York where the capitalistic system of the nation comes to a head.[14]

As it happens, Rauschenbusch, in his book *A Theology for the Social Gospel*, devoted considerable space to the reality of sin in the Creation accounts and the consequences of society's failure to recognize and treat its manifestations. And although he did not deal with Christian responsibility in the environment specifically, his wholistic conception of the comprehensive range of the Kingdom of God makes him a compelling figure for us to pay heed to today.

The factory took multitudes of people away from their historic homes. As the Industrial Revolution shifted to America, it beckoned them across the ocean to the land where "the streets are paved with gold." It alienated the workers from the source of production and most of its rewards. The worker no longer produced for himself but for the manager. He no longer drank from the milk of the cow in the barnyard or ate the vegetables from his field behind his dwelling because there was no longer a barnyard and there were no fields surrounding the Chicago tenements. The soil between his toes was now the city pavement that was oven-hot in summer and a sheet of ice in winter. And to make it, the worker's wife and his children had to join him at work on the factory production line. But in spite of the long hours and backbreaking toil, it was usually only the managers, owners, and bankers who made it to the golden streets.

The moon and the stars and seasons no longer ordered the working families' time—these were governed by clocks and factory whistles and the rhythm of production.

From Reality to Fantasy: FDR, Mickey Mouse, and Monopoly

Factories; mass migrations of people to work the iron horses of progress; profit and poverty; alienation from generations of soil and kin; some good times and a few Ragged Dicks who with "pluck and luck" made it big; an individualistic gospel that blessed profit; genuine opportunities for many who had come from European class-ridden ghettos; toil, tears, and exploitation for people of color who couldn't even make it to the bottom rung of the ladder—these are some of the fruits of the 1930s into the 1940s. This was the time, to quote Tennessee Williams,

> that quaint time when the huge middle class of America was metriculat-ing from the school for the blind. Their eyes had failed them, and so they were having their fingers pressed forcibly down on the fiery Braille alphabet of a dissolving economy. In Spain there was revolution. Here there was only shouting and confusion and labor disturbances, sometimes violent, in otherwise peaceful cities, as Cleveland, Chicago, Detroit.[15]

Isabel Leighton called the 1930s the Aspirin Age, which she charac-terized as a time of rapid social change, a fevered pace of life, the search for a cure-all that came no closer to it than a bottle of aspirin.[16]

Since the collapse of the stock market in 1929, banks continued to fail, and by the end of 1933, four thousand banks had closed their doors and 25 percent of the working population was unemployed.[17]

Natural disasters added to the hardships of the period. The early 1930s saw drought and winds create a dust bowl of the midwestern farming lands that, coupled with unfavorable economic conditions, forced many people to move westward. Later, in 1937, the Ohio River overflowed its banks, creating the worst flood in American history. Visual accounts of the period show families on the move in makeshift vehicles stuffed with possessions and underfed children, sometimes lining the highways, at other times camping at roadside Hoovervilles. The pathos of thousands of people leaving the land is described by John Steinbeck in *The Grapes of Wrath*:

> The people on top of the load did not look back. They saw the house and the barn and a little smoke still rising from the chimney. They saw the window reddening under the first color of the sun. They saw Muley standing forlornly in the dooryard looking after them. And then the hill cut them off . . . and the truck crawled slowly through the dust toward the highway and the west.[18]

The 1930s saw their share of mavericks, heroes, and even some fantasy superheroes. One of the mavericks was the one-time governor of Louisiana, Huey Long, who, for all his faults, built schools, roads, and public services and, racist though he may have been, was quick to name the unequal distribution of money as the major cause of social distress.

> When a man decides he must have more goods to wear for himself and his family than any other ninety-nine people, then the condition results that instead of one hundred people sharing the things that are on earth for the one hundred people, than a man through gluttonous greed takes over ninety-nine parts for himself and leaves one part for the ninety-nine.[19]

On March 4, 1933, Franklin Roosevelt became president, and on that day, too, the banking system came to a grinding halt. The mandate was clear: the country was in a mess, and Roosevelt had better do something about it. There was a flood of new legislation all aimed at the three Rs: relief, recovery, and reform. All in all, according to Arthur Schlesinger, the great achievement of the New Deal was the introduction of the United States to the twentieth century.[20] It was, according to Henry Steele Commager, "the culmination of a half century of historical development."[21]

Clearly, rapid change was taking its toll, and large segments of the populace simply could not adjust. They resorted to popular psychology and fantasy to get them through. Dale Carnegie—no relation to Andrew except in a shared glorification of capitalism—was foremost of the new brand of self-help authors. According to Carnegie, success is a matter of being valued by others and feeling important, though not necessarily through the accomplishment of material wealth (though, of course, money helps). First published in 1936, Carnegie's *How to Win Friends and Influence People* was an instant success, rapidly selling some seven million copies.[22] This was just one of many books with similar titles published during the period, and the message of them all was just the same: look inward and adjust.

And if self-help popular psychology couldn't do it, there was always fantasy. Mickey Mouse was the paramount cultural hero of the 1930s: Mickey was Everyman. (There was also Everywoman: Minnie Mouse. Minnie acting in the milieu of her age, stood inconspicuously behind Mickey. She encouraged him all the way and basked in the reflected glory of his accomplishments.) Mickey was at various times a cowboy, teamster, explorer, castaway, fisherman, inventor, Arab, sportsman, Gulliver, a circus clown, plumber, carpenter, magician, chemist, and farmer. His arena stretched from the Alps to the Amazon jungle.[23] Mickey embodied the image of what every American wanted to be. He was clean; he was innocent; he could defy time, space, and gravity; he could master the impossible; and most importantly, he was never outwitted.[24] Mickey was an international celebrity. His daring exploits were featured in comic strips and books in fifteen languages. He was the star of television's Mickey Mouse Club. For Britain's dowager Queen Mary, the movie bill wasn't complete without a Mickey Mouse cartoon, and Franklin Roosevelt demanded Mickey in the White House. It was said that Mickey would make "a lasting impact on mankind."[25] But not to be completely overshadowed by Mickey were other Disney characters of the period, each of whom carried their own distinctive messages. The Three Little Pigs stressed self-reliance, the virtues of conservative building, and the merits of keeping one's house in order.[26] Snow White was the young princess who was squeaky clean, beautiful, and naturally, white. The Seven Dwarfs were industrious little people who coaxed the unemployed to hum along with them, "Heigh ho, heigh ho, it's off to work we go," and, "Whistle while you work."[27]

The politicians of the day were offering economic solutions; the Dale Carnegies, adjustment and positive attitudes; and Walt Disney, magic kingdoms of escape. But—after all—wasn't life and fortune just a matter of throwing the dice? Monopoly, Parker Brothers' best-selling board game of 1935, stressed luck and chance with a slight tinge of moral obligation. Anyone could become a captain of industry and monopolize the public utilities or the railroads, and you need not be a Rockefellar or a J.P. Morgan to build a house—or even a series of hotels—on the Boardwalk or Park Place. And everyone had equal opportunity to pay the luxury tax or even to go "directly to jail" without collecting the $200 on the way. Hadn't life for millions become like a game of Monopoly: all just a matter of chance, a roll of the dice?

The Emergence of Mass Culture and Mass Unreality

On December 7, 1941, when the Japanese attacked Pearl Harbor and catapulted the American people into another war and another era, an obscure Harvard instructor, Howard Aiken, was already at work designing a machine that would figure mathematical problems beyond human comprehension and also have wide implications for the myriad of human problems. This ancestor of today's computer, along with introduction of television in 1947 and the transistor in 1948, contributed to the revolution in American technology and, most especially, to a revolution in characteristic modes of living.[28] These inventions were introduced in addition to those that had already altered peoples' modes of living, such as air conditioning and modern electric lighting. After all, if Clarence Birdseye could refrigerate and even freeze foods, people could also be refrigerated. Now people no longer had to while away hot summer's evenings on the city stoop or on front porches, chatting to their neighbors and watching the children play stickball in the street; they could sit inside a cool family room with a cold beer, watching the Yankees game. Or just wait a few years and the family need not even go out of the house to see a movie. All they needed to do was just rent a few films and relax in front of the VCR.

No one seemed to miss the hot evenings on the front steps and the easy camaraderie of the local neighborhood, the homespun jokes and the laughter. Nobody missed the Friday night outings to the neighborhood movie theater. It is only in retrospect that we begin to comprehend the many ways air conditioning and television have changed the shape of community and contributed to making us a more individualistic, isolated, and lonely people.

In the background of people's lives were the developments in atomic physics, which were even less understood and far harder for people's consciousness to comprehend. For the first time in human history, mass genocide had become a possibility. Laying aside for awhile what the existence of the bomb does to the human psyche, let us continue to look at the shifts in the physical world that people were attempting to absorb.

War and postwar prosperity brought more migration from farms to cities and from city centers to suburbs. The "organization man" and the suburb became distinct features of these prosperity years, and both were dependent upon a migratory population. As corporations expanded in size and power, their employees became more oriented around their jobs and their cars. When the corporations asked their workers to move and start up new branches, they moved. And the wife and children—whose opinion didn't really matter anyway—packed up the house and left without hardly looking back and with nary a tear—gypsies on the highway to the latest "promotion." After all, success was the goal and the organization the route. The organization was not just a job but a way of life, albeit a costly one. As William Whyte has said,

> As always, the way of success in an organization depends upon being aware that most of the decisions that affect one's destiny are made by others, and that only rarely will one have the opportunity to wrest control into his own hands.[29]

Willy Loman, Arthur Miller's fictional hero in *Death of a Salesman*, was successful in business but a failure in life. Sloan Wilson's nameless central character in *The Man in the Gray Flannel Suit* was an uneasy caricature of what middle-class suburban man was beginning to look like. The new men and new women were increasingly living in the Levittowns of the nation, extending mass organizational culture into a mass new way of living.

Ground was broken for the Levittown, Long Island, housing development in 1949. It serves as an early example of the principle of mass production applied to home construction, using prefabricated materials and assembly-line techniques, similar to those of automobile production.

Although there are volumes on the development of Levittown and what we might call the suburbanization of the United States, very little has been written about its social and religious consequences. But the brochure celebrating the twentieth anniversary of the Levittown in Pennsylvania is revealing:

> November 8, 1951, is a day to be remembered throughout America. It was a day the largest residential home builder in the world *changed the life of thousands of American citizens* [emphasis added]. It was the day that people of low and moderate income became a partner and sharer of the opportunities in the free enterprise system. It was a day a $100 deposit bought you a ranch type home, on a minimum lot of 70' x 100' in a proposed, fully landscaped, openspaced, garden community with paved roads and all utilities. It was a day, which five years later, would produce 17,311 homes and involve a population of over 67,000 residents. It was the day Levitt and Sons opened their sales office at the intersection of Route 13 and Levittown Parkway.[30]

Few would argue with the Levitts' boast that they had "changed the life of thousands of American citizens." Not a single American church or religious denomination could make that claim, but the Levitts did. And similar Levittowns—by whatever name—sprang up to surround every major American city. Suburban tracts were followed by condominium developments bearing such quaint names as Harbor Rest, Colonial Village, Georgetown Commons, Happy Acres, Deer Run. Then came the retirement communities and planned—read restricted—communities.

Most of these so-called communities share certain features. First of all they are not real communities; they have a natural look to them, but actually they are artificially created, with well-placed trees and flower beds and grass that is always green and sometimes with human-made lakes and ponds. The units all look alike on the outside (and often on the inside). You have to have at least one car to live there since there are no stores or public services, but they do generally have swimming pools, club houses, and increasingly, health clubs. Residents need not worry about safety, for the developments are protected by subtle and not so subtle social pressures regulating who can and cannot live there, and residents' councils keep out all but a few people of color. Some complexes cater to the affluent elderly, others to young families, and generally speaking, the elderly do not live in developments where there are children nor are children welcome in retirement communities (except for short visits to Grandma). For golfers, there are planned communities built around golf courses. Sailors can tie up their yachts in the tidy slips at the front of their units. There are vacation condominiums at Colorado and Vermont ski resorts, just an easy trek to the chair lift. And for the elderly of means, there are "life care" complexes so that Mother will never have to become a burden to her children, even unto illness and death.

But regardless of the type of planned community in which one lives, and even if one does not live in them, we all take forays out to the shopping mall. The mall, along with the Disneyesque amusement park, is probably the preeminant paradigm of our society, for it reflects our values and serves as a monument to what we as a people have become. I am grateful to Ira Zepp for starting me on a train of thinking on the phenomena of shopping malls and for his book *The New Religious Image of Urban America: The Shopping Mall as Ceremonial Center.*

In many respects all malls are alike. We get there in an automobile, and there is usually plenty of parking. If one is going to get a purse snatched, it will probably be right there in the parking lot, because upon entering the mall one enters a safe, crime-free world protected by unobtrusive guards. Usually there is Muzak softly playing in the background, and there are light, colorful banners and decorations appropriate to the season. And there is a natural look—just like the planned residential communities—with lush potted trees and gardens, flowers in their seasons, fountains and dripping water. There is usually a good bit of nostalgia designed to recreate a "ye olde English village" atmosphere and carts of trinkets or handmade leather goods or Navajo jewelry or Ecuadorian wall hangings. And food is available, from ethnic to all-American hot dogs. Increasingly, malls have replaced art galleries as exhibit halls for painting and sculpture. The shopping mall affords a certain amount of anonymity as well as a sense of comfort, security, and reassurance. Not many pan handlers will be found at the mall, nor the poor, because, although everyone can go to the mall, only those with money to spend can really enter into the experience. Malls are places to go when there is nothing else to do; they are places to take tourists and out-of-town guests. There is something there for every age group however young or old. And visiting a mall the day after Thanksgiving or Christmas is rapidly becoming an American tradition. They are good for a rainy day because they are inside; there are also heated in winter and air-conditioned in summer. Malls, according to Zepp,

> are contemporary versions of that age old combination of commerce and community. They will continue to fill the void created by our social institutions' failure in providing centers of ritual and meaning. . . . Quadrilateral architecture, calendrial rituals, replications of natural settings, and attempts to be people places and objects of pilgrimage, all illustrate *homo religiosus*. The shopping mall as ceremonial center, the shopping mall as "more than" a marketplace, is one way contemporary people are meeting their needs for renewal, reconnection, essential ingredients of religious and human life.[31]

Suburban housing developments, all manner of planned communities from the elderly housing complexes of Sun City to condominiums, vacation resort communities, and shopping malls— all these places share certain common features. They are environments that include those who can buy their way in. By the same token, they usually exclude the poor. They are generally safe. They look natural. In the case of housing developments, great pains are taken in planning natural-looking landscapes. In the case of shopping malls, the landscaping is brought in in the form of trees, gardens, and waterfalls because with inside landscaping almost anything is possible. Lush palms, figs, pandanus, and flowering tropical plants can grace a Minneapolis shopping mall where outside only hearty, northern hardwoods and pines grow on their own. The lobbies of Hyatt Regency hotels are also prime examples of inside landscaping as well as the foyers of many newly constructed urban office buildings. It all looks so natural, but nature was never so studied.

The artificial environment is carried to its ultimate extreme in the Disney parks. These parks—Disneyland and Disney World—are nothing like the old-fashioned Coney Island–Atlantic City style of seaside summer amusement parks with ferris wheels, roller coasters, and dodge-ems. Nor are they like the carnival that comes to the empty lot once a summer with its cotton candy, wheels of fortune, shouting old men who entice the crowd to win a Hawaiian lei with one easy toss of the ring over the Coke bottle, over-stuffed florescent teddy bears, merry-go-rounds, and laughing children who will finally agree to go home "after just one more ride."

When Walt Disney bought 244 acres of orange groves twenty-five miles south of Los Angeles in 1954 he said, "I wanted flat land *I could shape*" [emphasis added].[32] And Disney went on to explain the reason he erected a high embankment surrounding the park: "I don't want the public to see the real world. . . . I want them to feel they are in another world."[33] And a brochure of a walking tour of

Disneyland promises the visitor that the "world of today vanishes in a unique park. Here there is no present—only nostalgic past, hopeful future, and the miracle of times that never were."[34]

In the "nostalgic past" section of the park the visitor can walk down "Main Street," which is lit by replicas of old-time gas street lamps, take a trip on the *Mark Twain*, visit Tom Sawyer Island plus the Haunted Mansion and the Indian Village. "Adventureland" transports one on a jungle cruise down crocodile-infested waters past the Swiss Family Robinson's tree house surrounded by lush tropical plants filled with sweetly singing birds. In "Fantasyland" one can attend the Mad Hatter's Tea Party, ride the boats of "Storybook Land," or take a bobsled ride down the Matterhorn.

"Tomorrowland" is Disney's fantasy of America's future. Actually it is a glorification of the American present: nuclear submarines, an eighty-foot rocket, and a special exhibit called "America the Beautiful."[35]

The world Walt Disney created was a fantasy world, and the people flocked to it in droves. Those who could afford it, that is. Encouraged by the success of Disneyland, Disney Productions opened Disney World in 1971 in hot, sun-bleached central Florida. Here, centered around the Cinderella Castle and oversized Disney characters led by Mickey, the world's most celebrated mouse, visitors are treated to the spectacle of dancing bears, talking presidents, snarling ghouls, and pistol-packing frontiersmen. They are whisked on a sleek monorail train through the Magic Kingdom and the Polynesian Village, all in a location where, for a while at least, fantasy seems like reality.

And if Disneyland combined the mixture of nostalgia, nature, adventure, fantasy, and an idealized future, Disney World was all that to the maximum. In 1972, in Disney World's second year of operation, it was visited by 12 million—more people than lived in the state of Florida at the time and twice the number of foreign visitors who toured the United States that year.[36]

What is the significance and what is the message? Americans obviously did not and do not like the stark reality of modern life (such as described in chapter 2). In large measure, we have effectively given up any hope of renewing our natural world or of repairing our battered collective psyche. We are like the organizational people so aptly described by William Whyte back in the late 1950s, having long since given up any expectation that we can take control of the forces and events of our wider world. Seeking order and control in our lives, we have become a people controlled and held captive by circumstances beyond our control. Otto Rank described our condition thusly:

All our human problems, with their intolerable sufferings, arise from man [and woman's] ceaseless attempts to make this material world into a man-made reality . . . aimed to achieve on earth a "perfection" which is only to be found in the beyond . . . thereby confusing the values of both.[37]

It is all beyond us, or so it seems. So what we have done as a response to the chaos we can feel but not touch and change is to make a substitution. We have traded our uncertain reality for a fantasy reality. We have created our own version of nature; we have bought the Disney version wholesale—the version that is ordered and planned, the one that makes us feel comfortable and secure. And we have written off the rest.

In the next chapter we will attempt to seek an understanding of this huge sweep of events, circumstances, altered worldviews and life-styles, and their religious significance.

Ours is a life of spiritual chaos and bewilderment dangerously close to a state of madness akin to schizophrenia in which contact with inner reality is lost and thought is split from affect. . . . We pretend that our life is based upon a solid foundation and ignore the shadows of uneasiness, anxiety, and confusion which never leave us.

——Erich Fromm

5. Causes and Consequences

Telling Tales

The vignettes that follow are so common as to be mundane. The characters in the personal stories are my friends, neighbors, associates, and myself, so I changed their names to protect them. But under any names, just change the details a bit and adjust the surroundings and they are also you, your friends, your neighbors and associates. Some of the vignettes are from the daily newspaper—any paper, any day—in your paper as well as mine.

Every day Mike works at the boatyard that makes the most sophisticated submarines in the world. The finished submarine of one model will hold twenty-four missiles, each with the capacity to destroy 192 targets, and each one is seven thousand times more powerful than the bomb that leveled Hiroshima.

Every evening in the summer Mike lovingly attends to the vegetables in his organic garden, and in the winter he splits logs for the wood-burning stove. These activities and the country setting of his home give Mike great fulfillment because "a simple, honest life-style is healthy for the children."

Robert is president and chief executive officer of a company that provides technical support for the nuclear submarines and their weapons and communications systems—support, that is, for the submarines Mike builds at the shipyard a few miles away. The company has a workforce of 1,300. Robert feels that he is serving his country well through his company's work, for he readily points out that the Soviet navy is much larger than ours and more heavily oriented toward submarines than the U.S. Navy, since the Soviets have 369 submarines to the U.S.A.'s 139 (1988 figures). Because of the imbalance in numbers, he feels it necessary that the United States emphasize its technical superiority and give the highest possible priority to antisubmarine warfare. In 1988 Robert's company won $148 million in government contracts, and he is proud of that record. His company is important enough that its Dow Jones ratings are reported nightly on the local news and company activities are frequently refered to in the daily papers. Yes, people take notice of Robert's company.

Robert is also an active and loyal worker for his religious denomination. People take notice of that, too. He has been head of his church's statewide stewardship committee and an outspoken advocate for the benefits of tithing. Robert is very generous with his time, and his church activities obviously give him great personal satisfaction. Like Mike, Robert undoubtedly wants the best for his children.

A graduate student left the following notice at a campus gathering place:

> Help! I'm a 240-pound lesbian mother who has never had an orgasm. I am worried that my child will turn out to be heterosexual. . . . I have tried coke and self-fulfillment, why can't I make a commitment? I find everyone's body offensive, but then there are times when I just need someone to love.

We as a nation spend more money to feed our lawns than some countries spend on food for an entire population.

A South Dakota farmer told me that he keeps the cattle he'll slaughter for his household in a special pasture, and he never gives them dietary additives or hormones. He gives the same care to his household's chickens and vegetables.

But when he fertilizes the farm's fields, the potions he uses are so strong that he must wear a mask and protective clothing when he applies them. He wishes he didn't have to use the chemicals, but at least his own immediate family is protected from harm.

The Environmental Protection Agency projected that sixty-eight major metropolitan areas would miss the August 31, 1988, deadline set for compliance with the ozone standard specified by the Clean Air Act of 1970. Instead of progressing toward the goal of reducing ground-level ozone to safe levels, the country is losing ground.[1]

Unlike upper-atmosphere ozone, which forms a beneficial shield screening the earth from excessive ultraviolet rays, ground-level ozone is a serious public health hazard, particularly for those with respiratory or cardiac conditions. This is to say nothing of the long-term effects of ground-level ozone on the environment or its relationship to the gradual warming of the planet. The very hot, dry summer of 1988 with its excess of stagnant air has provided the ideal conditions for the formation and buildup of ozone.

If dangerous ozone levels were not enough, miles of beach from New Jersey to Massachusetts have been contaminated with medical debris that began appearing July sixth. A gruesome harvest containing needles and syringes, vials of blood (some of it testing positive for the AIDS virus), rubber gloves, and colostomy bags accompanies every high tide. All this, in addition to unusually high water-bacteria counts, has closed hundreds of beaches and is making the summer of 1988 one to remember, or forget . . .

Thousands of dollars and extraordinary effort may save the life of a dying three-year-old, and her mother makes a passionate appeal for help on the evening television news.

What would the same amount of money do for the millions of children who would be helped through routine nutrition, clean drinking water, and access to ordinary health care?

The church forum on AIDS and healing was being addressed by a member of her denomination's AIDS taskforce. Jane, we will call her, spoke very movingly about people she knew who were dying or had died of AIDS and attested to their remarkable courage in the face of impending death. Following her presentation, Jane was gently asked a question as to how she felt about teaching school children about the merits of old-fashioned chastity, and her reply was quite simply, "Any question about how one gets AIDS is both unnecessary and irrelevant."

The Canadian government is forcing the reduction of emissions and expects to achieve a 50 percent reduction within a few years. Such efforts are necessary because Canada estimates that 14,000 lakes in eastern Canada are already dead due to acidification and another 300,000 are threatened.

The United States during the Reagan administration has done nothing of a comprehensive nature to reduce emissions, although it is responsible for 50 percent of the acid rain falling in Canada.[2]

Sally and Joseph have been married for twenty years and are the parents of two delightful sons of whom they can be justly proud. Every Christmas they used to enclose with their greeting card the family's most recent photograph. We used to look forward to those annual contacts, if but through the mail, because Sally and Joseph and the children seemed to us like the ideal modern family. They both had productive careers and planned them in such a way as to allow time to enjoy the boys. They approached their responsibilities as parents intelligently and creatively. It was important to them that they encouraged the boys' athletic activities and their school projects. On weekends they went hiking in the forest and found time to play together as a family.

Stability has been particularly important to Sally because she knows from her own painful childhood past the trauma of living through parental discord and divorce. But she is seeking a divorce from Joseph. Sally and Joseph didn't ask their old friends for help. We wouldn't understand, she said. They tried to hold things together for the sake of the boys, but . . .

The layperson, bishop, and priest—all members of their church's national commission on foreign mission—were meeting at the New York headquarters to put the final touches on the commission's report to the national convention.

Having completed their work, they retired for lunch to a nearby restaurant with a panoramic view of the United Nations and the East River. On the way they passed several street people and beggars.

One of them asked for a donation, but the commission members just kept on walking.

At the restaurant, two members of the party just picked at their meal. They were on diets. The check came to $74.

In 1988 eight of China's thirty provinces were affected by a drought ravaging large tracts of central and eastern China, killing cattle and shriveling crops. Many rivers ran dry, and wells for drinking water yielded nothing but mud. In one province the drought was the worst in fifty years, in another it was the worst since 1578, back in the Ming dynasty. All in all, 9 million acres of agricultural land were harmed, destroying 70 percent of the peanut crop and 50 percent of the rice crop.[3]

It was July 1988 in Detroit, and there hadn't been rain since Mother's Day. For the fourth straight day in a row the temperature topped the one hundred degree mark. The grass in empty lots and backyards was tinder-dry. Forest fires raged out of control in South Dakota, Wyoming, California, Utah, Montana, and Arizona. In Yellowstone National Park, 40,000 acres of forestland burned down. It would rise to 450,000 acres before the summer was through.[4] In South Dakota the wildfire was consuming 1,000 acres an hour. When it got within three miles of Mount Rushmore—shrouding the presidential mountain with billowing smoke clouds—two thousand sightseers were forced to flee the area. It was far worse than the single day a month earlier when during one blistering hot, dry afternoon six thousand lightning strikes an hour had been recorded over the broad band of western states, sparking 421 fires.[5] The heat and drought were the worst ever recorded, and resulted in a 29 percent reduction in the year's corn crop.[6]

Back in Detroit, water was down to a trickle in thousands of Wayne County homes. But in Washington, the battle over Great Lakes water was just heating up on the floor of the Senate with the Great Lakes' states pitted against the Southerners who want Great Lakes water diverted to the Mississippi River. The Mississippi is so dry, the southern senators reported, that salt water is backing up into Louisiana's drinking water, and a thousand barges are stranded and grounded in the river. A Michigan senator replied that already in two years Great Lakes water levels had dropped some thirty inches. In the background of the debate were the voices of Canadians urging that the Great Lakes be left alone.

If this were not calamity enough, an American navy ship shot down an Iranian civilian airplane, killing all 290 passengers aboard. "A tragic accident," the President assured us. Ironically, the Navy captain who authorized the pushing of the button was one Will Rogers. Wonder if he's descended from the all-American, Oklahoma cowboy-philosopher of the same name who said, "I never met a man I didn't like."

Meanwhile the Sixty-Ninth General Convention of the Episcopal Church was meeting in Detroit. Deputies and bishops noticed the hundred-degree heat as they strolled from their air-conditioned hotel rooms to the air-conditioned convention center, but they wiped the sweat from their brows and just kept on walking.

When the Iranian airliner went down, the House of Bishops paused for prayer and sent a telegram of shock and sympathy. But other than that it was business as usual: the passing of the budget, resolutions concerning inclusive-language liturgies, women bishops, and, of course, there was the endless debate on sex. Should practicing homosexuals be ordained? Should same-sex unions be given the blessing of the church?

Sizing up the world and national events of the week and all that she had read in the *Detroit Free Press* about the Episcopal Convention, a waitress at one of the convention hotels commented over the breakfast she served one morning that "there sure is something odd going on around here."

Something Odd Going On

The telling tales share a common thread: something odd is going on, and things don't add up. In them, we see ourselves both as protagonists and as antagonists, as victim and victimizer, as partner in destruction and prophet of a new age. The pipefitter in the nuclear submarine shipyard is an ardent nature lover. Does Mike notice any discrepency between his work—the results of which would destroy nature—and his love for the environment?

Robert, the stewardship advocate, is also president of a research and development firm that is questionable in the eyes of some. Has he thought through stewardship that is responsible care and nurture of all of God's physical universe, and does he realize that stewardship also includes *the ways we earn our money* just as much as—if not more than—the ways we give our money away?

Robert's case is illustrative of the two worlds in which many Christians live. Not a person I know does not deeply appreciate Robert's work for his denomination. There is no question about the fact that we are giving more responsibly to the church as a result of Robert's efforts. He has raised some important issues with the people, and he has gotten results. Yet the same folk who benefit from Robert's work for his denomination refuse to deal with the realities of Robert's other world. They know little about it, and they like it that way. But the fact is that Robert does live in another world. He is a leader in a defense industry. His Fortune 500 company is a major employer in the area and a major receiver of government defense contracts, and he (and we) need to hold these two worlds together, painful though it may be to do so. All of us need to take to heart the grave convictions agreed upon by the member churches of the World Council of Churches, meeting at the sixth assembly held in Vancouver in 1983, in which it was agreed that work such as Robert's is "*contrary to our faith in Jesus Christ*."[7]

Although nuclear weapons had been condemned at previous assemblies of the world council, the Vancouver positions were the strongest yet.

> We believe that the time has come when the churches must unequivocally declare that the production and deployment as well as the use of nuclear weapons are a crime against humanity and that such activities must be condemned on ethical and theological grounds.[8]

And furthermore:

> Nuclear deterrence, as the strategic doctrine which has justified nuclear weapons in the name of security and war prevention, must now be categorically rejected as contrary to our faith in Jesus Christ who is our life and peace.[9]

There are many Roberts. Many of us live in two irreconcilable worlds just like Robert. And there are many of us who, on the face of things, have nothing directly to do with the armaments industry but who, nonetheless, benefit from the Roberts—like the clergy whose salaries come, in part, from Robert's financial contributions.

As we learn anew what it means to care for Creation and live into an ethic of responsibility, Christians are going to have to make some tough choices if they are going to be faithful.

The overweight graduate student needs someone to love, yet she is unable to make a commitment. The South Dakota farmer exercises care in how he grows meat and vegetables for his own family, yet he does not pass on that same care to the cattle he raises for sale to the general public. If he won't add hormones to his own family's cattle feed, why won't he take the same care for all his cattle? Why is there one way of growing grain for use of those closest to the farmer and another way for the grain that will end up on the nation's dinner table? Why is it that we of the northern, First World nations will feed our lawns and golf courses and generously water them while knowing that most of the world's people must endure neither proper nutrition nor adequate drinking water? Why is it, in fact, that the same people are capable of great good *and* great evil? Why are we—you and me—capable of extravagant acts of kindness and mercy *and* unconscionable evil?

Why do we respond to the mother who pleads for an organ for her baby on the evening news, even though after the huge expense of a delicate high-tech operation the baby will probably not survive a week anyway, while we ignore the cry of the poor for ordinary health care for all children? Why does the personal appeal to help just one baby move us? Every day thousands of children around the world suffer and die from diseases that are preventable or easily amenable to simple cures—like leprosy, polio, diarrhea, tetanus, typhus, and cholora, to name a few. On this issue Arthur Caplan, director of the Center for Biomedical Ethics at the University of Minnesota, said,

> Americans, while talking a good ethics game, behave as if it is not their problem. The lives of people in faraway places simply do not register on the scale of their consciences with very much weight. . . . It would cost those living in the developed world a few cents a day to save millions of lives each year by making simple vaccinations and other treatments more widely available to those in underdeveloped countries. We choose instead in this country to battle over how to expand access to transplants, artificial hearts, NMR scans . . . and other medical marvels to those who might marginally benefit from them.
>
> What can those in poor countries think of our ethics when their children die of diarrhea while we haggle over the morality of artificial heart implants.?[10]

What would it take to arouse our feelings for *all children* in need?

Why isn't the member of the AIDS taskforce just as concerned about how AIDS is contracted as she is about the care and consideration afforded AIDS patients? Since AIDS is 100 percent fatal, doesn't it make sense that school children understand how AIDS is caught and transmitted? And why are liberal folk reluctant to affirm the benefits of chastity and abstinence?

Sally knows from personal experience the pain of growing up in a home broken by divorce. Nonetheless she is seeking a divorce from Joseph. Is there nothing the couple could have done to remain together for the sake of the children? Is costly sacrifice for others an outmoded idea?

I have another friend, a Marshallese woman, Wilma, we'll call her, who is married to Lomaro, an incredibly cruel and sadistic man with whom she has had thirteen children. Wilma is under no illusions that Lomaro will improve. To her close friends Wilma readily admits that Lomaro is "bad" and "crazy." But when asked why she stays with him she simply said, "Because I am a Christian and a church member." Simplistic though that answer may sound to American ears, it is reason enough to keep Wilma faithful to Lomaro. Perhaps Wilma is endowed with a special strength that helps her to endure, but she is also a part of a culture where social restraint and religious commitment are still strong enough glue to hold families together. Sally is also a Christian, but neither her church nor her culture (our church and our culture) are healthy and strong enough to keep her family intact.

I was the layperson who, with the bishop and priest, walked by the beggars and street people en route to the expensive luncheon. Why did I do it? Was it that I didn't want to make a scene in front of my senior colleagues? I am an advocate for the poor, aren't I? Why do I so often fail to keep my actions consistent with my beliefs?

And how can church leaders huddle together, urgently discussing internal issues and passing resolutions dealing with internal denominational practice and policy while failing to look squarely at the critical, broad issues of our contemporary life? Has it not occurred to them and to us that the really urgent issues affecting all of our life and everyone else's are the ones rumbling in the background, those scarcely noticed by convention-goers? Hasn't it occurred to us that there is a relationship between how we care for each person in God's world *and* the physical aspects of God's environment? And hasn't it occurred to us that these broad issues of the environment, contemporary life, and international relations are also profoundly religious questions, against which all else pales?

As the Detroit waitress commented, "Something odd is going on. Things don't add up."

We share St. Paul's predicament: "I do not understand what I do; for I don't do what I would like to do, but instead I do what I hate. . . . For even though the desire to do good is in me I am not able to do it. I do not do the good I want to do; instead I do the evil I do not want to do" (Rom. 7:15, 18b, 19).

Is our current dilemma a cause or a consequence of our historical journey away from the natural world, a consequence of the Enlightenment and the Industrial Revolution, of the effects of our entry into the age of nuclear nightmare?

We can no longer afford to write off our dilemma as "the human condition," for it is now possible to end the human condition and every other living condition as well. The rest of the chapter will be devoted to looking at the ways our religious tradition has contributed to our alienation from the environment (but we won't leave it there, for in another chapter we will consider how our religious tradition can also be a stronger guide in bringing us back).

Causes and consequences are interrelated, but in an effort to understand them we will take a look at them separately. We will examine the church in retreat from the world, including the effects of a church turned inward; the desacralization of nature; and sin. We will consider these topics in the sure and certain hope that our understanding will point the way to corrective action so that together we may take responsibility for our common future and renew our efforts to care for Creation.

The Church in Retreat from the World

By all appearances, the earliest Christians were like the adherents of other Mediterranean religions and cults in that they were free to worship as they pleased. What made them distinctive was that they refused to acknowledge the divinity of the emperor and to do military service in the Roman Empire. Thus, they were brought into conflict with civil authorities, and as we know, persecutions and martyrdoms became the lot of our first-century Christian forebears.

So it is not surprising that by the second century Christian communities sought a distinctive identity apart from the secular society and began to seek purity and perfection by turning their backs on the world. The most dedicated members of early Christian communities became virgins and ascetics. In fact, virginity was coming more and more to be thought of as a requisite to a truly faithful life.[11] Rather than something to be ardently loved and prayed over, these purists saw the world and its occupations as distractions undermining the faith.

When the martyrdoms ended with the reign of Constantine, the monk replaced the martyr, and ascetic and monastic life came to be equated with, and on the same level as, martyrdom.[12]

By the fourth century, Christianity had become a worldwide movement and a divided one. There were tensions between the ordinary Christians, who married, held regular occupations, served in the army, and held public office, and the more rigorous virgins and ascetics who lived what was considered a more exacting, more holy, and more otherworldly life. As it evolved, the urban congregations simply could not contain the tensions and the double standard of these two distinct styles of Christian expression, so the virgins and ascetics broke off and left their city congregations to pursue holiness in the solitude of the desert. Turning away from the boisterous life of the cities, the ascetics renounced the world and self. As Owen Chadwick has described it, "The journey through the desert corresponds to the gradual stripping away of the natural life and the discovery of the spiritual life."[13]

But those who turned away from the world were not being faithful to Christ's intentions, for Christ never intended his followers to turn from the world, which is created and loved by God, but to work amid the structures of Creation in partnership with God. As Hans Küng has reminded us,

> Jesus did not preach—as the communities of the Qumran did—an ascetic withdrawal from the world; he founded no monasteries. Nor did he wish to separate off new areas of the "sacred" in time and place . . . distinct from the "profane" world.[14]

Not only was the world not affirmed, it was taken as suspect and a decided detriment to the full development of the faith. Futhermore, the idea of holiness evolved from its origins as a community affair to an individualistic quest for perfection. As I have expressed it in *The Liberation of the Laity:*

> From community to individual, from shared experience to solitary journey, from serving the social needs of the world to seeking lonely perfection, from holy to more holy. . . . It was a far cry from the early conception of the religious community as the priesthood of all believers, and it cast a long shadow over the subsequent development of the Church.[15]

With monasticism, which developed from ascetism, there evolved whole communities living apart from the world, pursuing a brand of spirituality distinct from that of ordinary Christians. Gnosticism, which also had roots in the second century, was an extreme and heretical version of Christianity turned away from the world. Gnostics did not acknowledge the world as being the Creation of God and went so far as to reject it as being thoroughly evil.

But leaving gnosticism aside, what we note very early on in the development of Christianity is a course of events that set the church apart from, over and against, the world. It was an adversarial relationship. And although ascetics and monastics have always been the minority of Christians in any age, they have at the same time represented an ideal and thus the moral tension between the development of an otherworldly spirituality as distinct from a world-affirming spirituality.

Retreats, quiet days, the revival of interest in the works of medieval ascetics and the desert fathers, spiritual direction—all these in our time hark back to a spirituality still dominated by the monastic ideal of renunciation. According to Pannenberg this "traditional penitential pietism, its lasting influence in Protestant theology and spirituality, is unfit as a truly contemporary form of Christian piety."[16] In *The Liberation of the Laity* I criticized such a spirituality as being detrimental to the development of a laity conscious of its ministry in and to the world, but now I would take it a step further and suggest that traditional monastic spirituality is detrimental to all Christians, laity and clergy alike, because it is not world-affirming.

According to a statement of the World Alliance of Reformed Churches,

> throughout the history of God's invitation to covenant relationship, and in our own historical moment, people have failed to respond to God who has called and is calling them to work with him in blessing creation. We are part of those people. Their failure is our failure. Their ambiguity about the world and its worth is our ambiguity. Their obstruction of blessing for the world is our obstruction.[17]

Our critical times demand the action of faith, which is expressed in the very heart of the crises of the world, for there Christ is truly present, pleading with us to renew Creation.

The Desacralization of Nature

The huge private jetliner came to a halt at Kennedy International Airport as reporters and dignitaries gathered to greet the pope on his first visit to the United States. The door opened as the roar of the plane's engines' gradually stilled. While leaving the plane, the pope waved to the crowd and flashed his characteristic warm smile as he descended the stairs to the tarmac. But before any formal greetings, the pope leaned over, dropped to his knees, bowed to the ground, and kissed it. It was a kiss to acknowledge the sacred ground and his—and all of humanity's—dependent relationship to it. This seemed an astonishing gesture because we are simply not used to seeing contemporary people symbolically illustrating relationship to the land, no less regarding it as sacred, holy ground.

If our well goes dry in the drought, I will be forced to recognize our basic dependence on water and the natural elements. But short of such an occurrence, I will probably continue to take for granted the water that comes without interruption from the well. Nothing has prepared me to actually believe that water is a sacred gift from God's sacred land.

Nor do I feel particularly dependent upon the weather and climate. In the cold I'll turn up the heat an extra notch or throw another log on the fire. In the heat of summer I'll just turn on the fan if it gets too hot. I can stay dry from the rain very easily. The sun and moon don't really matter; we have clocks so I don't have to read the sky. A tornado or a hurricane or blizzard will make me pay attention, but saving those extremes, I manage just fine, barely giving the natural elements a second thought.

In fact, natural elements don't hold much mystery anymore. We understand how storms work; furthermore, they are generally forecast so we can take precautions when necessary. We understand the sun and moon and their cycles, so they contain no mystery. People have walked on the moon, and they have assured us that it is not made of green cheese and that cows don't jump over it. Perhaps familiarity may not breed contempt, but familiarity may breed disrespect.

And what about animals? If cows were sacred in our culture, we would never eat a hamburger. If we really thought we were killing and spilling blood at every meal, we would either become vegetarians or die.

To a certain extent humankind cannot afford to be sensitive or even aware of its dependent relationship to the rest of the universe. If we allowed ourselves to fully understand the destructiveness implied by our simply living and eating—we would be overcome by despair and paralyzed into total nonaction. So a certain amount of insensitivity is both healthy and necessary. Jeremy Rifkin has called it desacralization: "Desacralization is a process that allows us to sever any relationship we might feel to other living things. By draining the aliveness out of things, we can pretend that our control and manipulation are of little consequence."[18] Our problem is that, since we have been able to understand, to control, and to master just about everything in the universe (or think we can, at any rate), almost nothing in the natural world can claim our respect; almost nothing is sacred.

Through growing into an understanding of the mysteries of the universe we have also objectified that which we have come to understand so that, in Martin Buber's terms, we stand in an I-It relationship to our surroundings, objectifying that which was once I-Thou. I-Thou, or I-You, suggests personification, relationship, mutuality; I-It, merely coexistence void of relationship.

Carrying on the thought of Buber, one might even say that the more "civilized" a people becomes, the more of the universe we understand and can master, the more also will we stand in I-It relationship in the cosmos. Not only that, in an I-It world, people also become objectified, deadened, as it were.

By contrast, people of so-called primitive cultures have not had sophisticated understanding and, thus, not the break with the natural world. As Octavio Paz, in discussing the ethos of Mesoamerican culture, has said, "The Christian attempts to save the individual soul, disconnected from the group and the body . . . while the Indian conceives of personal salvation only as a part of the salvation of society and the cosmos."[19]

Generally speaking, human beings have respect for that which they cannot master or understand. It is the other side of familiarity breeding contempt: lack of familiarity breeds respect. And furthermore, that which is not understood is usually veiled with fear and myth. As Ernest Becker has explained, "Man has always treated with consideration and respect those parts of the natural world over which he has no control."[20] And the converse: "As soon as he was sure of his powers the respect for the mystery of what he faced diminished."[21] Or according to Hocart: "As his superiority and mastery over the rest of the living world became more and more apparent [humankind] seems to have become more and more anxious to disclaim relationship with animals."[22]

A part of the desacralization of nature is the demythologization of nature. What humankind cannot understand comes to assume an aura of fear, mystery, and myth. One of the costs of technological understanding is a loss of imagination—that wonderful capacity to make myths and to believe them.

It is like children's fairy tales. Where reason ends, there imagination takes over. Thus, fairy tales are the stuff of the young, who still lack knowledge. But when we grow up, we put away childish things. This is why certain scholars have taken it for granted that fairy tales originated during the childhood of humanity and that they are expressions of totemism, taboo, and primitive thought.[23] It is not for nothing that Jesus said, "Let the children come to me because the reign of heaven belongs to such as these" (Matt. 19:14). Heaven belongs with those who have the simplicity of spirit to just believe—like children.

But the afternoon has passed, and the evening is at hand. There is yet a little time (we hope) before the bell tolls. Can we use it to relearn how to kiss God's holy ground? Can we grow beyond knowledge and familiarity and contempt into ardent love and respect for every human being and every aspect of the natural world? Can we uncover myths and believe them? Can we open our minds to mystery and imagination? Can we allow a little child to lead us? Rifkin says it succinctly:

> To end our long, self-imposed exile; to rejoin the community of life. This is the task before us. It will require that we renounce our drive for sovereignty over everything that lives; that we restore the rest of creation to a place of dignity and respect. The resacralization of nature stands before us as the great mission of the coming age.[24]

Dehumanization

Of all the isms of our day—from industrialism to racism—the overarching one is nuclearism. Nuclearism transcends race and culture, nationality and locality. Aside from living and breathing and conducting our universal daily habits, nuclearism is the preeminent common factor that binds all people together everywhere. It binds humanity in one gigantic question mark. Some of us, to be sure, are more aware of our existential uncertainty than others, but nonetheless, we all live our lives in the shadow of a terrifying nuclear mushroom cloud too vast for the wildest of anyone's imagination to begin to comprehend let alone absorb into consciousness. And it is that cloud looming in the background that determines much of our behavior as human beings.

Nuclearism, according to the psychiatrist Robert Jay Lifton, foremost pioneer in the area of the psychological effects of living in the nuclear age, is the disease underlying our dis-ease:

> For nuclearism is a general twentieth century disease of power, a form of totalism of thought and consequence particularly, if paradoxically, tempting to contemporary man as another of his technological replacements for his waning sense of reliability and continuity of life.[25]

If one agrees with the centrality of the notion of nuclearism, then we begin to understand much of human behavior as an adaption to nuclearism. Here all the defense mechanisms we know so well—the meat and potatoes of every basic high school psychology course—come into play. Namely, in the face of real or perceived danger—actual or psychic danger—the human being fights, flees, denies, projects, rationalizes, compartmentalizes, introjects, sublimates. And the function of defense mechanisms in every case is to hold self together and keep anxiety at bay.

But the prevailing defense mechanism that in various ways employs the others is dehumanization. As such it is aptly called a "composite defense."[26] Dehumanization has also been called depersonalization, loss of affect (that is, loss of the ability to feel), and psychic numbing. Dehumanization has been described by Lifton as well as by Bernard, Ottenberg, and Redl, and most recently by Konrad Lorenz and G. Clarke Chapman. Lorenz, better known for his human and animal studies of behavior, has described the condition as the "waning of humaness."[27] It is Chapman's opinion that nuclearism has, in effect, become a religion in and of itself.[28] And certainly Lifton would agree, for he is quoted as saying, "Nuclearism is a secular ideology in which 'grace' and even 'salvation'—the mastery of death and evil—are achieved through the power of a new technological deity."[29]

Few would deny that the apocalyptic aspects of Christianity have been intermingled with the ethos of nuclear distructiveness, like the popular bumper sticker that began to appear several years ago. I saw several dozen of them one Sunday morning in the parking lot of a large, rural Minnesota Roman Catholic Church. The slogan reads, "When the rapture comes this car will have no driver."

Dehumanization manifests itself in numerous ways. Its prevailing characteristic is just what the word suggests: dehumanization, a loss of the conscious capacity to feel, the blunting of emotion, the failure to experience the full range of emotional depth and to connect with others. It is not that basic feelings have disappeared but rather that they have been cut off before coming to realistic expression. Dehumanization expresses itself in what we would best describe as a flat personality. It is the inability to express real joy, heartfelt laughter; it is evident in those who feel sad but are unable to cry, in those who have long since forgotten the art of just having fun.

Bernard, Ottenberg, and Redl equated the increasing prevalence of dehumanization with the increasingly pervasive nuclear ethos of the times.[30] Carl Jung, years earlier, noted the phenomenon and felt it to be a side effect of civilization:

> What we call civilized consciousness has steadily separated itself from basic instincts. But these instincts have not disappeared. They have merely lost their contact with our consciousness and are thus forced to assert themselves in an indirect fashion. Contemporary man [and woman] is blind to the fact that, with all his [and her] rationality and efficiency, he [and she are] possessed by "powers" that are beyond his [and her] control. His [and her] gods and demons have not disappeared at all; they have merely got new names. They keep him [and her] on the run with restlessness, and vague apprehensions, psychological complications, an insatiable need for pills, alcohol, tobacco, food—and, above all, a large array of neuroses.[31]

There is a lonely, isolating quality to dehumanization. The dehumanized person has a longing to know others and to be known by them but is unable to communicate; he or she cannot reach out in healthy ways to others. He or she needs and desires to be nurtured by the generous company of friends and family. But since the dehumanized person is unable to nurture, the relationships most dearly wanted dry up on the vine or are inappropriately expressed and the individuals involved remain alone and isolated. Absent among the dehumanized is the capacity for imagination. Since imagination usually involves thinking into future time, and since future time is now called into question, the only course left for the would-be creative dreamer is fantasy. And fantasy, by its very nature, has no reality.

The North American Anglo, such as myself, looks longingly at the vitality evident in many ethnic and aboriginal cultures: the charm of a backyard Fourth of July barbecue in one of Newark's Latino neighborhoods, with hamburgers and chicken roasting on an oil-drum grill, music, unfettered laughter, children running everywhere; or perhaps the laid-back life of outer-island Micronesians as they carry on their daily round of fishing, copra-making, anticipating and celebrating village festivals in the warm and generous company of family and friends. Recall the appeal of Democratic presidential hopeful, Jesse Jackson. Jackson stood apart from the other candidates by his sheer energy and passionate vitality, his aliveness. The dehumanized Anglo is drawn to and captivated by their *authenticity,* a characteristic sadly missing from most of our contemporary milieu.

No wonder the idealistic young rebel. They rebel against the lifelessness of their parents, their hollow values, and their hollow religion. But most of them will rejoin their parents a few years down the line; they, too, will join the ranks of middle management and disappear into the vast company of the living dead. These former flower children, campus reformers, and peace activists have already become upwardly mobile and materialistic and, on the surface at least, proud of their imported German luxury cars repleat with leather bucket seats, tinted glass, and car telephones. Make no mistake, they have worked hard. They have talked their way into M.B.A. programs just as they have clawed themselves up the spiral to success. They sport designer fashions and relax in Jacuzzis in front of "adult movies" plugged into home VCRs. When it's convenient for them, sometime after they've purchased the right house in the right suburb, they will consider giving birth to a child or maybe two. They will dress the child in designer child-ware and surround him or her with toys and the material symbols of their class. And when the child crys out in despair en route to day care, "But I just want to be with you, Daddy," Daddy will wearily toss the toddler another mechanical toy and reply, "Tomorrow, Son, tomorrow. Just let me get through today's business trip." And like the generation of their parents before them, these young executives will resort to alcohol, drugs, all manner of destructive behavior, and quick kicks to get it all *today.* But make no mistake, those caught in this young urban professional syndrome are not to be condemned—pitied perhaps, but not condemned. Rather, considering them begs *the underlying question:* Why have they become reabsorbed into the very life-style they once repudiated?

These so-called Yuppies are merely the most obvious and exaggerated examples of how the great majority of us in middle-class America deal with the unspeakable dread with which we are all surrounded and entangled.

Dehumanization is the ultimate pervasive response to the predicament of our times. It is a destructive defense because it provides a convenient means of avoiding responsibility.

Sin

By the time Martin Luther nailed his Ninety-five Theses to the church door on All Saints' Day in 1517, thus ushering in the Protestant Reformation, intelligent Christians had had enough of sin. Medieval theologians had brought the feudal penitential system of sin and its confession to a fine art. A whole corpus of moral theology had evolved in which sins were carefully categorized and cataloged. Once a corporate matter and a community affair, during feudal times sin became a personal morality matter. And as the notion of sin had changed, so too had practices of confessing sins. Confession, which during the patristic period had been public and unusual, now had become a private and precious activity, and the whole penitential system with private confession became an area of clerical domination and abuse. Along with it came the means by which penitents could pay—quite literally—for their sins, that is, by abolishing penalties through the buying of indulgences.[32] So it is no wonder that Luther's insistence on faith, not works, not sin—was welcome news. And, according to some opinion, since the end of the seventeenth century there has been little further development in the doctrine of sin in Protestant traditions.[33]

With indulgences eliminated in the Roman Catholic Church, sin and its confession remained, for the laity at least, a fairly harmless activity. Anglo-Catholic Anglicans in the late nineteenth century incorporated Roman Catholic forms of private confession into their tradition, but mainline Protestants, for the most part, virtually eliminated the doctrine of sin from popular religious teaching.[34]

By the 1920s it was becoming patently clear to many Protestants that the churches' accommodation to the gospel of wealth was only leading the church and the world to a dead end. Fortunately, there were voices emerging that insisted Christianity must be shaped, directed, and corrected by the ethical standards of the Reign of God. Failure to do so would continue to render the churches powerless for anything save self-preservation.

A part of the restatement of the ethical standards of the Reign of God for the technological era was the need to unpack the doctrine of sin from its feudal past and give it contemporary application. The apologists for the Social Gospel believed that a new appreciation of sin was absolutely tied to gospel-inspired social reform, for as Rauschenbusch said in *A Theology for the Social Gospel* (of which four chapters are devoted to sin): "A serious and humble sense of sinfulness is part of the religious view of life. Our consciousness of sin deepens as our moral insight matures."[35] And Reinhold Niebuhr, author of *Moral Man and Immoral Society* (1932), felt it necessary to reinstate the doctrine of Original Sin because, as he explained, "the real dimension of the problem of faith and the common life is obscured in secular and in liberal Christian morality because there is no appreciation of the fact of sin."[36]

Two apt definitions of sin came out of the 1937 Oxford Conference on Church, Community, and State (a forerunner of the World Council of Churches), one by Reinhold Niebuhr in the paper already quoted and the other the work of John C. Bennett. Bennett's definition of sin and his placing of sin in its wider social context is most helpful: "Sin [refers] to any form of evil which is the result of moral failure—including both deliberately chosen evil and evil which is the result of blindness which can be traced to selfishness, inertia, insensitivity."[37]

This was an excellent beginning, and every assembly of the World Council of Churches, from the 1948 meeting in Amsterdam onward, has dealt with sin in one way or another but especially in relationship to national defense and war. But the churches simply did not follow suit. At best, it has been a side issue, receiving little direct attention of itself.

But if the churches have failed in this generation to address the issues of sin—as distinct from injustice and war where the record is better—social scientists, under another guise, have dealt very directly with it. Some of them, particularly Jung and Menninger, have referred to sin as not only a moral or psychological problem, as one would expect, but as a distinctly spiritual problem as well.

The question is begged: What is sin? What is evil? How about aggression? What do we mean by the death instinct, by destructive drives?

Bennett has called sin a form of evil; social scientists, on the whole, have not. Nonetheless, from Freud to Fromm, the great classical psychiatrists and psychoanalysts have all, in one way or another, given a great deal of time and attention to what we of the religious community call sin. Freud called human aggression "the greatest hindrance to civilization."[38] Other social scientists have made their contributions: Konrad Lorenz, a naturalist, illustrated that of all the carnivores (that is, animals that kill other species to obtain their food), all of them also have innate inhibitions against killing members of their own species, except the rat and the human being. Lorenz reasoned that since people are poorly equipped physically for killing—having neither adequate teeth nor claws—they do not have built-in inhibitions against killing other people.[39] Ernest Becker contended that humankind's natural and inevitable urge to deny mortality and achieve a heroic self-image is the root cause of human evil: "The thing that makes man the most devastating animal that ever stuck his neck up into the sky is that he wants a stature that is impossible for an animal; he wants an earth that is not an earth but a heaven."[40] But, according to Becker, the price for this reckless ambition "is to make the earth an ever more eager graveyard than it naturally is."[41]

Stunned by the horror of the tremendous violence inflicted by American soldiers in the My Lai massacre during the Vietnam War, a prestigious group of social scientists met in San Francisco to exchange papers on the subject of evil and particularly on issues of how social sanctions for evil came to exist and how people cooperate in doing harm or in failing to prevent it. This was one of the occasions for which Robert Jay Lifton and Bernard, Ottenberg, and Redl developed their ideas about dehumanization, and they associated the phenomenon with evil. Their papers and other conference papers were published under the title *Sanctions for Evil: Sources of Social Destructiveness.* Of the eighteen papers on the subject of evil, not one was delivered by an identifiable member of the religious community. Ironically, the conference was held in space provided by Grace Cathedral in San Francisco. The corporate nature of sin has simply been a nonissue of the churches for several decades.

But there are a few notable exceptions, such as the Sojourners Community in Washington, D.C. One of its founders, Jim Wallis, has criticized the church for its preoccupation with individual sin while ignoring the full panorama of social sin and social evil. According to Wallis,

> in their preoccupation with individual salvation, twentieth century evangelists very seldom point to national values or institutions as evidence of sin. Sin is located only in the individual heart, not in the economic system. . . . Armed with a largely personal definition of sin, modern evangelists have lost the capacity to relate the Gospel to the collective evils of our time.[42]

But Wallis and the Sojourners Community are exceptions.

My question is, where have leaders of the Christian community been while social scientists—right through this century—have devoted so much energy to the issues of sin (by whatever name)? Why have mainline Christians been conspicuously absent from the dialogue?

The pious North American Christian will protest these questions. The pious North American Christian will point to the revival of individual spiritual direction; the revival of interest in medieval mystics, who certainly did stress the reality of sin; the revival of Anglo-Catholic private confessions.

But I say that the church has continued to reduce and trivialize sin as individual transgression and that all of the above are but signs of both the individualistic understanding of faith and practice and the individualistic understanding of sin and repentence; all are part of the "my spiritual director," "my confessor" motif; all are turned inward away from the world.

The church turned inward, just as Niebuhr had warned, has become so unaccustomed to taking leadership in the social affairs of the world that it seems to have forgotten how to speak to the cosmic issues of our time; it has forgotten how to name sin as sin. Worse still, the American church of today fails even to have a developed conception of the fact that the destruction of people, the destruction of the environment, wars and rumors of war are *profoundly religious matters.*

Perhaps it must be foreign voices who tell North American Christians the truth about ourselves. Perhaps we are too close to ourselves to see ourselves with any clarity. Lesslie Newbigin of the Church of South India, for example, said,

> The Church has lived so long as a permitted and privileged minority, accepting relegation to the private sphere in a culture whose public life is controlled by a totally different vision of reality, that it has almost lost the power to address a radical challenge to that vision and therefore to modern western civilization.[43]

And John DeGrunchy, a South African who, as such, knows all too much about evil at first hand, has said that "the Church must, in large measure, accept responsibility for this inner, spiritual collapse of European culture which reached its nadir in the rise of Nazism but is omnipresent in secularism."[44]

A prerequisite to the church regaining its voice and passion in society will be that it truly accepts the fact that God permits evil because God also has the power to draw good from evil and that evil and good, sin and blessing are—in every way—two sides of the same coin.

The Deadly Duel

Uncertain as to whether or not God's Creation is good; a history of piety historically dominated by the monastic ideas of renunciation of the world for the sake of the kingdom; a church that has reduced and trivialized sin to individual transgression; a church that has long since lost its nerve and retreated from engagement with the critical issues of our time—all these add up to a church that, in effect, has given up on the world.

Ours has become a world, according to Küng,

> in which man builds up, forms and transforms his own world. It is a world—and this applies particularly to the material world of science,

but also increasingly to the biological and anthropological world, of biophysics and genetics, of psychology, sociology and economic sciences—which make up a closed system of phenomena and functional relationships, which are capable of being experienced, calculated, experimented with, predicted and manipulated, a closed system in which the entity known as God no longer appears. . . . It is a technological world in which the arts, law, social life and all areas of culture are no longer deduced from or positively formed according to religious interpretations and objectives, but planned, constructed and realized by man [and woman] in a completely secular way.[45]

Having given up the hope and the will to transform God's Creation, yet retaining the normal human need for order and control in temporal matters, mainline churches have settled for second choice: transforming themselves and their structure. Christians unwilling or unable to transform the world are concentrating their attention on the world of the church, which they can manipulate and control.

And since the church is still dominated by its clerical minority, which is—by the nature of its calling—institutionally oriented, the effects have been disastrous for both the church and the world. For, however much we may give lip service to the ministry of the laity, the shape of laypersons ministry in the world is still misunderstood by both clergy and laity alike.

A passive laity, which still, by and large, interprets its role as service within the institution while neglecting the world to which all ministry is intended to be directed, has allowed the church to drift into a backwater and a dead end.

Without the necessary lay corrective, we have stood silent and permitted the clergy to focus the energy of the church inward to the structural life of the institution. Every mainline religious tradition has their list of insider—mostly clerical—issues that the clergy have made the main agenda for their denominations. In the tradition of which I am a part, the Episcopal Church, the issues currently receiving the lion's share of attention are those of nonsexist language in liturgy; women bishops; the revival of the office of the vocational diaconate (another way of reclericalizing the church); and matters of human sexuality (the ordination of practicing homosexual people, the blessing of same-sex unions, etc.). No doubt the great majority of Episcopalians never heard of postmarital unions until they were informed about them by the church's Standing Commission on Human Affairs and Health. The point is not the merit of the particular issues but rather that they are all matters of doctrine, style, and polity and, as such, matters that shape the internal structures of the institutions. To be sure, peace and justice resolutions continue to be debated and passed, but center stage is decidedly occupied by internal matters that affect the minority of membership in the church.

All the while the laity do have issues they feel the church is not adequately addressing: They are concerned with family values and the world of their childrens' future. Many feel the church has failed them in its failure to stress the importance of personal moral values. They are worried about illegal drugs and alcohol, teenage suicide. There is scarcely a parent of a high school student who is not worried about some aspect of his or her child's education. Most people are distressed about the declining quality of human life and the condition of the environment. We have become afraid of our technology; we are choking on our waste, and we are upset about it. Even members of the military and defense industry workers will admit to being worried about the stockpiling of nuclear weapons and the continuing development of a new generation of weapons. Real though these issues may be to the laity, they are largely silent, and they do not press them on the church. In part, this is because the laity have learned the lessons of their place only too well. But also they are so intimidated by the issues of our time that they can hardly conceptualize them enough to ask the searching questions the issues require. They should be more bold. They should take to heart what Frederick Douglass said a century ago, that "if there is no struggle, there is no progress. Those who . . . renounce controversy are people who want crops without ploughing the ground."

So what we have in progress in our congregations is a deadly duel between clergy and laity in which the partners may touch but not penetrate each other's armor. The laity may listen to the clergy's concerns about internal matters; yet they keep the lid on the issues that concern them most, afraid to jar the lid even a little. The laity could express themselves in the community of faith, but they prefer to remain silent for fear of causing division. The clergy could, for example, comment on the way members of their congregation earn their living, yet do not do so for the same fear of causing division. Both sides hold back to avoid division within the community; both hold back because both are implicated in the issues which confront society and the church. There is blood on the hands of both clergy and laity. And both are caught in the paralysis of knowing that the dilemmas of our day are so immense, so complex, the individuals involved so nameless and faceless that no one can see his or her way through the morass in order to know where and how to act in society to make a difference.

It is a deadly duel: viewing each other through mesh masks, touching armor and only touching the surface, dancing around an open sanctuary in perfect yet lifeless symmetry, "and [we] ignore the shadows of uneasiness, anxiety and confusion which never leave us. We do not know the answer because we have forgotten to ask the question."[46]

The man who sat on the ground in his tipi meditating on life and its meaning, accepting the kinship of all creatures and acknowledging unity with the universe of things, was infusing into his being the true essence of civilization.
——*Luther Standing Bear*

Within the traditions, beliefs and customs of the American Indian people are the guidelines for [human]kind's future.
——*Vine Deloria, Jr.*

6. Listening to the Land: The Witness of Native Cultures

The American Indian Movement and Us

The 1960s in the United States were idealistic days. Students for a Democratic Society (SDS) was taking over university administration buildings and demanding that students have a place in the decision-making processes on their campuses. This situation was an offshoot of the citizens' demand to become an active part of the nation's decision-making process that would—it was hoped—extricate us from the unpopular Vietnam War. Coming hard on the heels of the civil rights movement, when Stokley Carmichael was crying, "Black power," on the one hand, and others were attempting to continue Martin Luther King's methods of nonviolent protest, on the other, these were the heady days when university students questioned the lifestyles of their parents, the relevancy of their religious denominations, and the morality of their nation. Virtually everything—once taken for granted—was meat for examination, and virtually everything was found wanting.

It was more than youthful rebellion, for, indeed, much *was* wanting in the white, middle-class, corporate American culture that included double-talk and double lives, deceit and dishonesty. Amid such ferment, those searching for wholeness and authenticity saw their ideal in the Native American. Indians fit the bill exactly. True, contemporary Indians bore the marks of having been run off their native lands and relegated to reservations; they wore the scars of having been "relocated" to urban job-training programs. Virtually

99

every Native American had been subjected to efforts to "American-ize" and "acculturate" them, which, translated, means that Indians had become pawns in a systematic assault to stamp out all Indian-ness—that is, native language, tribal customs, habits, and life-style, and native arts. But throughout what amounted to cultural (and actual) genocide, the Indians, nonetheless, had retained a con-tinuity with clan and land that many regarded as highly desirable and worthy of emulation.

> The Lakotas and Cheyenne were a people whose theology, whose government, whose relationship with the environment was far advanced over that of the whites who first made contact with them. Ideally . . . this still is true today . . . it is time for whites to turn to the Lakotas, to my own Cheyenne people, and to Indian people as a whole, not only to learn what the relationship of man [and woman] to the en-vironment should be, but also to understand the very nature of man [and woman].[1]

And as Black Elk, an Oglala Sioux, said,

> We should understand well that all things are the works of the Great Spirit. We know that he is within all things: the trees, the grasses, the rivers, the mountains, and all the four-legged animals, and the winged peoples . . . and even more important, we should understand that he is above all these things and peoples. When we do understand all this deeply in our hearts, then we will fear and love, and know the Great Spirit, and then we will be and act and live as He intends.[2]

But the Native American model posed a number of problems: Native American people were in the throes of their own movement for civil rights and a rebirth and recasting of their own distinctive cultural identity. As such, they understandably did not have much interest in being used yet again to meet someone else's ends. Native Americans, in any case, felt it was not their contemporary state that made them attractive to this generation but rather a romantic vision of the Indians of past days. Also they knew that Indians have a culture to be lived and an oral tradition to be passed down from generation to generation, an ethos not easily transmitted outside the tradition.

Nonetheless, many Americans, Native Americans included, have been convinced that a key to returning the land and people to right relationships with each other and all members of the cosmos lay embedded in native culture. Vine Deloria, Jr., a leading Native American spokesperson, expressed the opinion that

> within the traditions, beliefs and customs of the American Indian people are the guidelines for mankind's future. . . . The lands wait for those who can discern their rhythm. . . . The future of mankind lies waiting for those who will come to understand their lives and take up their responsibilities to *all* living things.[3]

Yet Deloria was under no illusions, for he also said that "the particular tragedy of the Indian movement is that it has never been able to influence the intellectual concepts and values by which Americans view the world."[4]

This was in 1973 at the height of the American Indian movement and, of course, Deloria was proved correct. Although Indian tribes have been highly successful in the reclaimation of tribal lands (one of the goals of the American Indian movement), they have not yet succeeded in providing an alternative worldview that would have any chance of influencing the great majority of Americans to change.

Vancouver Voices

Unrealistic though it may appear, the idea that the holistic understanding of Creation held by those of indigenous cultures needs to be shared by the wider society will not go away, as the sixth assembly of the World Council of Churches (WCC) amply attests. Justice was the unifying theme of that 1983 Vancouver meeting that asked the World Council's member churches to engage in a conciliar process of commitment to justice, peace, and the integrity of Creation,[5] and furthermore, to the idea that there could be "no peace among people without peace with nature."[6]

In describing the WCC's new phrase—Peace, Justice, and the Integrity of Creation—and new program called for at Vancouver, Preman Niles, head of the Peace, Justice, and Integrity of Creation process explained that

> the term includes ecological and environmental issues but goes beyond them. Its central thrust is on the caring attitude towards nature. It tries to bring together the issues of justice, peace and the environment by stressing the fact that there is an integrity and unity that is given in God's creation. What this means will become clearer as we continue in the various struggles for life, and realize more fully that we live in an interdependent world of complex relationships and delicate balances . . . that justice for the poor and hungry is tied up with issues of justice for the land. To ignore the integrity of creation is finally to destroy all that sustains us. In essence it is a call to a new life-style that is based on stewardship and compassion rather than on mastery and exploitation.[7]

Integral to the process has been a consultation "to draw in several understandings of creation that are normally neglected, especially aboriginal, American Indian, Maori/Polynesian."[8]

The WCC defines "indigenous peoples" as tribal people who hold traditional worldviews that include attempts to live in harmony with the whole of Creation. Examples of indigenous peoples cited are American Indians, the Dalits of India, Maoris, aboriginal Australians, Africans, and tribal Asians.[9]

The remainder of this chapter will be an exploration of the lessons aboriginal cultures can teach us if we will but learn to listen.

Living with the Land

The Native American has a different attitude toward the land then most members of the dominant culture. It is an attitude of acceptance, of appreciating the land as it is, of accommodating one's self to the land, of blending in with it. Take the Hopi, for example:

> The Hopi . . . working on the land does not set himself in opposition to it. He works *with* the elements, not *against* them . . . He is in harmony with the elements, not in conflict; and he does not set out to conquer an opponent. He depends upon corn, but this is part of mutual inter-dependence; it is not exploitation.[10]

The Indian looking over the gathering shadows in the buttes and draws, in the ripples and undulations, on the wide expanse of prairie, absorbs its beauty and feels quiet contentment. That's it. The non-Indian might look at the same view in a different way: How is it useful? How could it be productive? Would irrigation make the land more profitable? Does oil lie under the prairie cover? What about minerals? How could the land be changed to fit human purposes and human utility? It is as Jim Swan recounts in the state of Oregon: "To a timber company, the Oregon ridge I visited was a mature stand of timber with so many board-feet of valuable lumber. To the Klamath tribe, this has been a place of spiritual power for centuries."[11]

Or in South Dakota:

> The Lakota and other Plains tribes see the Black Hills as the heart of the Earth Mother. . . . Large mining corporations say the Black Hills should be mined to use the uranium for electrical power and weapons, and the Honeywell Corporation wants to use a portion of the region to test new weapons.[12]

Barry Lopez recounts a conversation he had with a Yup 'ik hunter on St. Lawrence Island in which he was told that what the Eskimo fears most about us is the extent of our power to alter the land, and thus the Yup 'ik call us "the people who change nature."[13]

The native eye sees the land as it is; the Anglo eye sees production, possibility, profit. It is the difference between being and using, between accommodation and utilization.

In citing the difference between the native attitude and ours, Lopez uses the Eskimo as an example:

> One of our long-lived cultural differences with the Eskimo has been whether to accept the land as it is or to exert the will to change it

into something else. The great task of life for the traditional Eskimo is still to achieve congruence with a reality that is already given.[14]

This native outlook is very reminiscent of the thought expressed in the *Tao Teh Ching*. Product of the ancient Chinese civilization of the mid-third century B.C., the Tao says,

> The world is a sacred vessel not to be acted on.
> Whoever acts on it spoils it;
> Whoever grasps at it loses it.[15]

Unlike the person of native culture, the Anglo historically has become accustomed to living with duality, with departmentalization, and with boundaries. It is part of the duality developed in the churches through which certain places, certain people, certain experiences were—and are—considered to be sacred. The rest secular. We set boundaries between people and the environment, between nations, and between me and we. Tradition and centuries of practice have conditioned the Anglo to think with a divided mind and to feel with a divided heart. But if we are going to correct our fragmented condition, nation, boundary, duality, and individuality will have to give way to our commonality as people and citizens of the universe. As Stanley Rowe, a member of the Saskatchewan Environmental Society, has said,

> How can the world of nature and the community of peoples with their national economies be harmonized? Posing the question this way suggests that the two are separate. But not so. Humanity, the human species, exists and is supported within the world of nature. And I mean that not figuratively, but literally . . . we are animals living inside an ecological system . . . it is all of *one piece*.[16]

To live with the land is to live in harmony with every aspect of Creation and with the Creator; it is to experience a unity and a continuity with time and eternity. We of the dominant culture might learn from our native brothers and sisters who are closer to the land, for "this archaic affinity for the land . . . is an antidote to the loneliness that in our own culture we associate with individual estrangement and despair.[17]

Secular as Sacred

The great Creator of the world—whether called Usan, Wakan, Wakantanka, Great Spirit, or by any other name—is present in every aspect of the created order. To be sure, some locations, such as the Black Hills, Chief Mountain, Blue Lake, Mount Shasta, were imbued with special religious significance. But generally speaking the manifestations of the Creator God are everywhere. God is intimately involved in God's Creation, therefore everything and every being and everywhere is sacred, nothing secular. Chief Seattle, in a letter to President Polk in 1852, explained the holiness of all of God's Creation revealed in the web and unity of mutually dependent relationships.

> Every part of the earth is sacred to my people. Every shining pine needle, every sandy shore, every midst in the dark woods, every meadow, every humming insect. All are holy. . . .
>
> We know the sap which courses through the trees as we know the blood that courses through our veins. We are part of the earth and it is part of us. The perfumed flowers are our sisters. The bear, the deer, the great eagle, these are our brothers. The rocky crests, the juices in the meadow, the body heat of the pony and man, all belong to the same family.
>
> The shining water that moves in the streams and rivers is not just water, but the blood of our ancestors. . . . Each ghostly reflection in the clear waters of the lakes tells of events and memories in the life of my people. The water's murmur is the voice of my father's father.
>
> The rivers are our brothers. They quench our thirst. They carry our canoes and feed our children so you must give the rivers the kindness you would give any brother.
>
> . . . the air is precious to us, the air shares its spirit with all the life it supports. The wind that gave our grandfather his first breath also receives his last sigh. The wind also gives our children the spirit of life. . . .
>
> . . . the earth is our mother. What befalls the earth befalls all the sons of the earth. This we know: the earth does not belong to man, man belongs to the earth. All things are connected like the blood that unites us all. Man did not weave the web of life, he is merely a strand in it. Whatever he does to the web he does to himself.
>
> One thing we know: our god is also your god. The earth is precious to him and to harm the earth is to heap contempt on its creator.
>
> . . . What will happen when the buffalo are all slaughtered? The wild horses tamed? What will happen when the secret corners of the forest are heavy with the scent of many men and the view of the ripe hills is blotted by talking wires? Where will the thicket be? Gone! Where will the eagle be? Gone! And what is it to say goodbye to the swift pony and the hunt? The end of living and the beginning of survival. . . .
>
> We love the earth as a newborn loves its mother's heartbeat. . . . Preserve the land for all children and love it, as God loves us all.
>
> We are part of this land, you too are part of the land. This earth is precious to us. It is also precious to you. No man, be he Red Man or White Man, can be apart. We are brothers after all.[18]

Furthermore, God is continually being revealed in the forms of nature: in the rising and setting of the sun; in hills and mountains and in the shape of the land; in natural forms—the changing shape of the moon; in seasons and storms; in animals—buffalo and birds, deer and elk and bear. Walking Buffalo, a Stoney Indian of Canada, expressed it as follows:

> We were on pretty good terms with the Great Spirit, creator and ruler of all. We saw the Great Spirit's work in almost everything: sun, moon,

trees, wind and mountains. Sometimes we approached him [the Great Spirit] through these things.[19]

More recently, Peter Powell, a Roman Catholic priest who spent his formative years working among the Cheyenne and Lakota and, indeed, found his priestly vocation among the Indian people, said the following with regard to sacred and secular:

In Lakota life there is no difference between sacred and secular as presently exists in Anglo-American life and learning. For the Lakotas and Cheyennes all creation is sacred, all creation is filled with supernatural life . . . Sacred Powers assume forms that human beings can recognize. Thus the Sacred Powers may appear as animals, birds, or natural forces. . . . This is a sacred world, a world filled with supernatural life and power. The Earth, the Mother of the People is a supernatural person.[20]

So, in effect, when Native American people are cut off from the land, they are also alienated from God. "To give up the Earth, their Mother, would also cut them off from Wakan Tanka and from all the Sacred Powers whose spiritual presence fills all creation with supernatural life."[21]

Sharing

It takes a long time to make ready a Marshallese feast on Mili Atoll, for the fish, the chicken, pork, taro, breadfruit, and coconuts have to be gathered and prepared by the cooks and then divided equally among all participants. If it is the feast at the schoolhouse marketing the end of Education Week for all three hundred of the islanders, or a family party of a dozen or so, the process is the same: everyone, children included, shares equally. In fact, *share* and *divide* are one and the same word in the Marshallese language, and indeed *everything* is divided and shared. When rain has not been plentiful and water catchments at some family compounds have gone dry, it is expected and assumed that those without water will help themselves at compounds where there are larger supplies. The fish caught off the coral reef are amply shared among those who need them; when the field-trip ship is slow in coming to the atoll and supplies of rice and sugar are low, what little the people have is passed around.

The stranger or visitor is a particular recipient of generosity. Gifts and parties will accompany her arrival and also mark the end of a visit. Visiting eight family compounds in a day will mean having eight meals served. To be wealthy in the Marshall Islands is to have more to share.

Sharing and giving are high virtues among the Marshallese, and it is a trait shared by other aboriginal peoples, for example, the Ojibwa.

One of the prime values of Ojibwa culture is exemplified by the great stress laid upon sharing what one has with others. [Through sharing] a balance, a sense of proportion, must be maintained in all interpersonal relations and activities. Hoarding, or any manifestation of greed, is discountenanced.[22]

In Lakota tradition, occasions of happiness were occasions for the giving of gifts. Also, when a Lakota died, the family held a giveaway to distribute the property of the deceased and other family possessions as well. Luther Standing Bear described the giveaway following the death of his infant son in 1905:

I had a lumber wagon and top buggy, with two beautiful teams of horses for them. Both were new vehicles, and the harness was spick and span. The lumber wagon I loaded with groceries, meats, bead-work, blankets, dry goods, and many other articles of value. The buggy was filled with beautiful bead-work. On the side of it we hung the full costume of my little boy who had died—buckskin suit, bead-work vest, moccasins, and little blankets. These were given away in remembrance of him . . . my wife and I walked away with practically nothing.[23]

The custom of giveaways was still alive and well when I lived and worked on South Dakota Indian reservations in the early 1960s. At that time I learned of many cases of people giving away virtually all their household possessions.

For the Marshallese and the Lakotas, as well as for people of other aboriginal cultures, less in material possessions is equated with more in virtue; generosity is equated with contentment.

How does the North American of the dominant culture explain such sharing and generosity, which is sadly missing from our modern life? It is probably related to the basic aboriginal worldview that human beings live—or ought to live—in reciprocal relationships with all other beings and with the natural environment. The person of a native culture gives gifts out of gratitude for the plenteous gifts he or she has already received. Ernest Becker describes it succinctly:

Unlike us, [so-called] primitives knew the truth of man's relation to nature. Nature gives freely of its bounty to man[kind]—this was the miracle for which to be grateful and beholden and give to the gods of nature in return. Whatever one received was already a gift, and so to keep things in balance one had to give in return to one another.[24]

Humans and Other Beings

The person of an indigenous culture apprizes his or her place in the scheme of nature and regards it with an attitude of awe and humility. Human beings, in every sense, owe their lives to others, and they are physically sustained by others all the length of their days. This concept is amply expressed through the aboriginal person's relationship with the animals killed for food.

Traditionally, the lives of the Eskimo were dependent upon the seal or whale or polar bear—depending upon where the Eskimo lived. The lives of the Cheyennes and Lakotas depended upon the buffalo; the deer was similarly important to other western American tribes. The people owed their well-being to the animals (just as these animals owed their lives to "lower" animals of the natural world).

Hunting and fishing, which so-called civilized people do for sport, were—and are still—the means of survival for aboriginal people. The person of an aboriginal culture does not hunt and fish for amusement or recreation nor does he kill for the sake of killing. He has too much respect for animal life than to treat it wantonly. When an animal is killed, it is for the purpose of providing life for people. And the hunter will kill only what he needs for his family or clan. The hunter killed, yes, but he did so soberly and for a concrete purpose because, according to Lopez, "the hunter saw himself bound up in a sacred relationship with the larger animals he hunted. The relationship was full of responsibilities—to the animals, to himself, and to his family."[25] And according to Alice Fletcher, "the spirit of apology is offered over a slaughtered animal, for the life of the one is taken to supplement the life of the other, 'that it may cause us to live.' "[26]

The Wintu people, who once occupied most of the valley of the Sacramento River in California, were similarly respectful of the deer. The Wintu hunter "kills a deer only when he needs it for his livelihood, and uses every aspect of it, hoofs and marrow and hide and sinew and flesh. Waste is abhorrent to him, not because he believes in the intrinsic value of thrift, but because the deer has died for him."[27]

A spirit of mutual obligation is also evident among the Ojibwa, who are—or were—hunting and gathering people.

> Since the various species of animals on which they depend for a living are believed to be under the control of "masters" or "owners" who belong to the category of other than human persons, the hunter must always be careful to treat the animals he kills for food or fur in the proper manner.[28]

Best known among Americans is the historic relationship between the Lakota and the buffalo. Since their lives depended upon the buffalo, the Lakota, mindful of their indebtedness, regarded the buffalo as possessing an aura of particular holiness because they believed that Wakan Tanka (God) revealed himself through the buffalo: "The Great Mysterious [God] reveals his generosity through the buffalo. For the buffalo . . . provides the people with food, clothing and shelter."[29] In addition to food provided by the buffalo, clothing and moccasins were made of buffalo hides; also tipis. Buffalo bones and horns were used to make tools and implements; sinews for bows came from the animal's fibers; the stomach was used as a container for water; buffalo chips were used as fuel. Indeed, the buffalo provided the Lakota with everything needed for life, and there was very little waste. Therefore,

> the buffalo was approached in an attitude of respect and prayer. Before the great tribal hunts . . . prayers were offered by the holy men as well as individuals among the people themselves. After a hunter killed a buffalo he usually offered a prayer of thanksgiving both to Wakan Tanka, who gave the buffalo to the people, and to the buffalo himself who had given up his life so that the people might eat and live.[30]

The Common Good

In common with members of early Christian communities, native peoples have a well-developed notion of the common good. Indeed, this nation was built on the assumptions of goodwill and public cooperation among the people, and these were considered basic to the maintenance of a strong and healthy nation. As James Madison, chief architect of the Constitution, stated in one of the Federalist papers, "[T]he public good, the real welfare of the great body of people, is the supreme object to be pursued . . . no form of government whatever has any other value than as it may be fitted for the attainment of this object."[31]

Unfortunately, Madison's ideal of the common good has not withstood the test of time. Robert Bellah reported in *Habits of the Heart* what we know to be true: that Americans have become an individualistic people intently interested in individual experience and intimate relationships; that we have become a people for whom self-reliance has become a virtue and competition a means to obtain personal goods and goals. But the aboriginal ideal, as well as practice, has been different, for according to Roxanne Dunbar Ortiz, "what was good for the community was good for the individual and what was good for the individual was good for the community."[32]

Living in the community of tribe, clan, and family, there were rights and responsibilities that were commonly understood as forming the basis for the well-being of the group. The well-being of others received a higher consideration than personal well-being; the well-being of the tribe came before the welfare of the family.

> In Lakota thought, it is always fitting and proper to put the needs and rights of the tribe first. For, in doing so, the individual man or woman is acting as a human being should act. He or she is functioning as a true member of the people.[33]

Our contemporary society desperately needs a revival of the time-honored idea of the common good, for according to Bellah, as the twentieth century has progressed, that understanding [of the common good] so important through most of our history, has begun to slip away from our grasp. . . . Madison, Tocqueville, and Debs . . . believed that the survival of a free people depends upon the revival of a public virtue that is able to find political expression. . . . Is it possible that we could become citizens again and together seek the common good in the post-industrial, post-modern age?[34]

Learning Lessons from the Land

As Native Americans continue to press for the reclaimation of tribal lands and more aggressively seek to see that hunting, fishing, and treaty rights are honored by the dominant society, the Anglo will be forced to reckon with the modern Indian and, hopefully, to retire timeworn and romantic images of Native Americans. The Native American has a great deal to say to the dominant culture right now at this juncture in our history, and not only the Native American, but aboriginal peoples everywhere. The Native American has a wholistic attitude of relationship with the land and with every natural aspect of the nonhuman world. The Indian people have a great gift embedded within their culture that all people need if we are going to survive into the next millenium. Will the Native American people share their gift? Perhaps more pointedly, will we of the dominant culture have the grace to receive it?

Owanah Anderson, a Choctaw, is weary. In acknowledging a new interest on the part of Anglos in Indian spirituality, she is fearful that the non-Indian world will look only to Native American spirituality as ceremonial rites (sweat lodge, pipe ceremony, sweet grass, and the like) while ignoring the far more important "native concept of noncompartmentalization which holds there to be no separation between the secular and the sacred."[35]

The World Council of Churches in its activities to engage the member churches in the issues of justice, peace, and the integrity of Creation has suggested that

it is more and more clear that the Kingdom of God (Mark 1:15) is not merely a relationship between human beings and God that has happened or will happen at a particular time. Rather the Kingdom of God is the space where God reigns. It must be understood as a metaphor for all Creation. In this context "repentance" *(metanoia)* must be informed by the Old Testament notion of "return" *(shub)*. It is a return to God and to the space where God reigns as Creator, that is, to a proper relationship of all creatures to the Creator. It is a return that brings one back into harmony and balance with God and with the rest of Creation. Thus [for us] repentance opens new possibilities for understanding ourselves and our place in Creation. For indigenous peoples repentance must involve a return to their spiritual source, that is to their land.[36]

Native Americans who consulted with members of the World Council's Justice, Peace, and the Integrity of Creation process have already criticized the ordering of those words because they believe that right relations with the land is a precondition for justice and peace. As Carol Hampton has said,

> Our understanding of the world tells us that creation comes first and we must acknowledge the priority of creation. Justice comes out of the wholeness of creation. Only when we have accepted or have allowed a just creation can there be peace. The team [of Native Americans consulted] recommended that the name be changed to "Creation, Justice and Peace."[37]

The first Americans can teach all Americans right and just relationships with all people and with all aspects of God's Creation. The survival of our land and every land and the survival of our faith may depend upon how well we listen to and heed the wisdom of native voices, for as Vine Deloria, Jr., has said, "Christianity itself may find the strength to survive if it honestly faces the necessity to surrender its narrow interpretation of history and embark on a determined search for the true meaning of man[kind's] life on this planet."[38]

So may it be . . .

We are the curators of life on earth; we hold it in the palm of our hands. Can we evolve spiritually and emotionally in time to control the overwhelming evil that our advanced and rational intellect has created?

——Helen Caldicott

7. Toward an Ethic of Responsibility: Ten Commendments

The summer of 1988 may have been the turning point. Debris-filled and contaminated beaches in a summer of extreme heat and drought, solid scientific reports that pollution may be altering the climate, and evidence that ground-level ozone may be adversely affecting even healthy people—these factors have contributed to a widespread unease.

Sewage treatment, recycling plants, emissions control, safe disposal of industrial and agricultural toxic wastes, conservation, shifts to clean and renewable energy sources—these had been written off as merely the concerns of a small minority of kooks, hippies, and idealistic environmentalists. It used to be said that such projects and issues lacked voter appeal. Those seeking to preserve the environment and to retain wilderness areas were considered elitists, out of touch with the practical realities of life. Their pleas to save the environment were regarded as luxuries the nation could ill afford. Environmentalists who felt that natural resources should be preserved were pitted against those with money and public opinion on their side who pushed for the development of natural resources. The environmentalists on one side and the developmentalists on the other, it seemed that there was no way the twain would meet, and the weight was with the developmentalists.

Then came the summer of 1988, during which environmental protection became a part of each political party's platform and message and both presidential candidates incorporated issues of the environment into their party's acceptance speeches.

Lester Brown, president of the Worldwatch Institute, said of the summer of 1988, "We may be crossing a perceptual threshold. . . . We're seeing an elevation of public awareness. . . . Finally [people are] starting to understand that we can kick nature only so long before nature starts kicking back."[1] And Jessica Tuchman Mathews of World Resources Institute said, "Ten years from now one may look back on this time as a seminal moment when people began to look quite differently at these problems."[2]

At this seminal moment in learning to care for Creation, the following Ten Commendments are offered as building blocks toward an ethic of responsibility. They are intended to stimulate the imagination and action, for like St. Basil the Great, "I want creation to penetrate you with so much admiration that everywhere, wherever you may be, the least plant may bring to you the clear remembrance of the Creator."[3] For behold, God said, "It is good," and thus worthy of consideration and ardent love.

1. Repent

In learning to care for God's Creation, nothing less than repentance is required as a first step. The Greek word *metanoia* is translated both into repentance and conversion: repentance—turning about; conversion—turning away. Repentance and conversion are two sides of the same coin. Repentance is a precondition for conversion. It is saying no to one set of values, beliefs, or actions and then saying yes to another set. It is like the three denials in the examination of candidates at the beginning of the Service of Holy Baptism that are followed by three affirmations. (The person being baptized first renounces Satan and the forces of wickedness that rebel against God, renounces the evil powers of this world, and renounces sinful desires that draw one away from God. *Then* he or she affirms and accepts Jesus as Savior, agrees to put his or her whole trust in God, and agrees to follow and obey God.)[4] In a similar way, when one becomes an American citizen, allegiance to the former country must first be denied before pledging allegiance and becoming a U.S. citizen. After months of applications, security checks, and interviews, in the end it is a matter of saying no to one nation and yes to another. The yes cannot occur without the prior no. It's like that with repentance and conversion. Conversion cannot occur without repentance.

What does repentance entail? Obviously no one is going to repent unless there is an awareness of wrong doing. In this case we are not talking—in the first place—about the wrong done by one individual to another but rather the wrongs I and my society commit against the environment and against humanity in general. It is asking the questions, What is the wrong (or evil, or sin) in God's world? and, How have I (or how has my group, community, or nation) contributed to it?

One comes into the awareness of wrongness in a number of ways. It might be the terrible summer of 1988 when nothing natural seems to work in the manner we have come to expect (the rain doesn't come, the air is polluted, fish are dying in the oceans, and there is no relief from the intense heat). Or it might mean looking at one's own life and circumstances, as I have attempted to do in chapter 2, and determining the many ways the declining quality of life is affecting you or your family and associates.

Or pick up any newspaper wherever you are and count up the news stories about the negative aspects of the environment. Just today, for example, a typical August day, my newspapers have at least ten items concerning the environment: "On an Island of Ice in an Arctic Odyssey"—about chemical pollution in Arctic waters that had hitherto been considered relatively pure; "The World's Debt to 12 Million Refugees"—about the world's uprooted millions who still wait for permanent homes; "The Green Revolution: How Much Further Can It Go?"—about the limits of the world's grain harvests and the castrophe that will occur if we have a second year of drought; "How the Lung Reacts to Ozone Pollution"—about microscopic lesions and scar tissue that develop even in healthy individuals and may cause permanent damage; "Low Level Waste"—about Connecticut's need to find a low-level nuclear waste disposal dump within the next eighteen months for the thirteen hundred tons of low-level nuclear refuse produced every year. And so on. The titles change, but every day the theme is the same. Count up the articles about the environment, read them, ask yourself what they mean to you. Do the same with items on the evening television news.

Environmental issues are more obvious than the nuclear issues. They are in the news more, and we can see and feel damage to the environment all around us. In other words, something has happened and is happening, and it is now becoming very apparent to everyone. Not so in the case of nuclear issues. Moreover, we cannot afford to wait so that we can see and feel the effects of nuclear damage as we have done with environmental matters. A small nuclear accident, a missile detonated in error demolishing a large population area, for example, would cause the same shift in consciousness that occurred with the drought of the summer of 1988. It would be something for everyone to see or feel. But such would not be possible, for no nuclear weapons accident would be small,

and any survivors would be full of radiation sickness and fully occupied with burying the dead. But there are ways to educate oneself
about nuclear affairs. Every state has local and statewide nuclear
weapons freeze organizations. These organizations know the size,
power, and cost of the nuclear arsenal. There are also such national
organizations as Beyond War, International Physicians for the Prevention of Nuclear War, and Global Education Associates, as well
as the resources of most denominations' national headquarters.
Swords Into Plowshares, by Arthur J. Laffin and Anne Montgomery,
contains an excellent listing of peace and disarmament groups and
how to make contact with them. *Planethood* by Benjamin B. Ferencz
and Ken Keyes is similarly helpful.[5] The easiest way to get a broad
picture of the facts and statistical analysis of each nuclear country's
armaments—their firepower, defense budgets—plus their contrasting
figures for social spending worldwide is to get a copy of a sixty-page
booklet full of graphs and charts that is revised every two years. It's
title is *World Military and Social Expenditures.*[6] It's author, Ruth Legar
Sivard, is a highly respected economist who was formerly head of
the economics division of the U.S. Arms Control and Disarmament
Agency. In my opinion, every Christian ought to have Sivard's booklet
in his or her home right beside the Bible and the daily newspaper,
and these ought to be read and pondered together every day.

After determining how each of us is immediately affected by
living in our damaged environment, and how our life-style and that
of our nation contributes to the picture, we need to consider how
each of us personally contributes to the tearing down of God's
Creation.

Where and how do I live? Do I have a larger house or apartment
than I actually need? How about the gadgets and appliances? How
many televisions do I have? Do I need all of them? Do I have a
second home? Do I consume more than my fair share of energy?
How many cars does my family drive?

How do I—and my family members—make their money? Stewardship is just as much—if not more—a question of how I earn my money
as how I spend it. Does my job or profession contribute to the building
up of God's world or to its continued destruction? As I have said
previously, "Christians should neither work in industries producing
questionable products nor serve on such companies executive
boards (unless by doing so they can effect healthy change)".[7] Are
my fellow workers treated justly and with dignity? Some industries,
and businesses' products are not questionable, but production
workers are exploited.

What about consumer products we buy? The Berne Declaration
Group in Switzerland says that consumer goods and issues ought

to be evaluated according to three basic criteria: health, ecology, and justice.

> Does the product damage your health (or that of the producers and/or processor)? Did producing it contribute to pollution of the environment or draw excessively on non-renewable resources? Did the producers (as far as one can know) receive a decent return for his/her labor?[8]

Education, the development of awareness, and sensitivity—these are the goals for examining our world and our involvement in it. Awareness and sensitivity are just as necessary as education. Merely learning facts and even changing one's mind, however, are of little use in themselves. According to Vincent Rossi,

> What is really needed is a change of heart. Heart! Not just a change of mind. . . . We know that human nature does not respond just because the mind changes. An untransformed heart is the reason why our actions don't bear fruit. It is easy to be ecologists in our *heads*. . . . Change of heart is necessary. We have got to change our hearts if we are going to change anything.[9]

As questions are asked and explored, a consciousness as to the way things actually are will develop and, it is hoped, a moral restlessness and tension. Realistically, of course, life-styles, consumer patterns, and employment cannot be changed overnight, but there is *no chance of change whatsoever* without a willingness to ask the questions and the cultivation of a developing sensitivity to the issues.

A change of heart, a turning about, a shifting from wrongness to rightness—this is repentance. Awareness of wrongness must lead to an attitude of repentance. This repentance, according to Hans Küng, is

> not an outward repentance with sackcloth and ashes, but a radical and total inward change of the entire man [and woman], towards God [and] radical faith is possible *only* through repentance which recognizes personal guilt and the need for grace and expresses a readiness for radical fulfillment of the will of God [emphasis added].[10]

And John Bennett says the same: "Something deep within us must be changed, and when we have chosen [and continue to choose] courses which we know to be . . . destructive, we need nothing less than moral conversion."[11]

Repentance, conversion, turning from, and turning to: it is a turning to a new way of living into God's reign of wholeness and love of Creation. It is not a set of rules, not prescriptions, not self-righteous piety, not judging others harshly but, rather, seeing the mote in one's own eye first. It is a style of awareness and a style of sensitivity to everything and everyone that make up the world around us. It is an attitude and a habit of living, an attitude of dawning awareness of the goodness of God, and each other, and all of God's Creation, and it is a habit of humbly living out the awareness of God's reign. It is closing the gap between what we believe *ideally* and how we act *really.* According to Leonardo Boff,

> being converted does not consist of pious exercises, but rather a new mode of existing before God. . . . This reversal in one's mode of thinking and acting is to be life-giving; it is to lead a person to a crisis and to deciding for the new order that is already in our midst, that is Jesus Christ himself.[12]

Let us repent so that we may live.

2. Talk

Let us take off our masks and talk to each other. Let us drop our protective shields and discuss together the grave issues of our time as they impact our lives. Churches have a golden opportunity to be safe zones for the sharing of the controversial, anxiety-provoking, and threatening issues of our time. There is hardly a parent who is not fearful in some way about the world our children are inheriting. A recent letter to a local newspaper said it well:

> My children's education is important to me. Not only because of my responsibility as a parent but because education is the only real defense against all the trials that my children will have to fight their way through.[13]

Thousands of workers are caught in intolerable working conditions with no ready escape. Just yesterday a New York City bus driver told me that he was worried about himself and his fellow drivers who work in constant noise, pressure, and the endless traffic of vehicles and people always in a hurry. For the men and women who spend their working lives behind the wheels of Manhattan's buses, the heart attack is an all too present reality. "You see it builds up; it goes here [pointing to his chest]. You can't scream at the riders or yell at the wife when you go home. It just goes here." And we parted with his final words, "I got two more years of it. I hope I make it."

Thousands of people are worried that the environment where they live may be killing them. For years, government officials assured the people living around the Feed Materials Production Center at Fernald, Ohio—a uranium-processing plant—that there was no health risk from the low levels of radiation the plant was emitting into the air. But the people could see otherwise. They tested the water in their wells, and it was toxic. They had the evidence of cancers developing in themselves and in their children. They saw their friends and neighbors dying too young; they had the evidence of their women delivering more than the usual number of stillborn babies.

How do the people handle their legitimate concerns for their children and families, their anxieties about their jobs and the environments where they live? What do they do with all their anger and dis-ease?

The churches have succeeded in being a moral voice in some situations of injustice in society. They have been moving forces in the establishment of shelters for the homeless, food pantries, and soup kitchens. They were vocal in their opposition to the Vietnam War. They are currently vocal against U.S. intervention in Nicaragua. But the moral voice of the church has been selective. The churches have failed miserably to address the ordinary social issues of our day that affect the ordinary members of our congregations.

People are falling apart because of the conditions of society, not because they are crazy or "sick" or neurotic. It is the *society* that is crazy, sick, and neurotic, and by and large the churches have failed to recognize it. And failing to recognize where the blame lies, they have done very little to ameliorate the causes of our deep unrest. Since the end of World War II, our churches have been dominated by the CPE therapeutic model (Clinical Pastoral Education). Pastors became therapists; churches became places where parishioners—particularly women—took their "problems." And what the pastor offered was a sympathetic ear and help in "adjustment." As the CPE model developed and caught hold, a course in Clinical Pastoral Education became a requirement many denominations set for those aspiring to be ordained. John Snow, in *The Impossible Vocation,* has traced the development of CPE to its current dominance.[14] It is a disturbing account.

The therapeutic model promotes adaptive personal behavior rather than behavior that challenges and addresses the deficiencies that caused the stress in the first place. And it is an odd twist and an ironic footnote that for all the clergy's knowledge of psychology and human behavior, for all their CPE, their personal lives are falling apart just as surely as those of their parishioners. Moreover, sin has been relegated to a mere problem, salvation trivialized, and blame abolished.

> The whole reason for adopting therapeutic values is to remove blame from human interaction so that human beings can look objectively at their behavior and its motivation and alter it to reduce conflict and suffering.[15]

So we adapt our behavior and conform to the behavioral norms of our parishes. We do not ask the searching questions, nor do we challenge each other or the norms of our world that tear at our gut. Yet George Gallup, Jr., in reporting the Gallup organization's most recent poll, "Unchurched America Ten Years Later," commented that if mainline churches continue to lose members it will be because of *their lukewarmness,* not because of their treatment of controversial issues.[16]

Obviously, change is in order. We need to talk with each other about the dilemmas of our lives and the ways they affect us personally. To do so we will need to trust that the fabric of our Christian communities will be strong enough to contain the conflict and the sharing of opposing viewpoints that will be an inevitable part of talking with each other. Churches are uniquely suited to the cross-fertilization of viewpoint and opinion both about our work and the pressing issues of our world. All the "telling tales" at the beginning of chapter 5 ought to be meat for discussion in the safe zone of the parish—environmental problems, the plight of farmers, medical and business ethics, national fiscal priorities, local political affairs and campaigns, hunger and homelessness, rising real estate prices, the quality of local public schools, international affairs, hopelessness and despair among our youth.

Issues that are most contradictory, most tense, most deeply troubling ought to get a hearing in our Christian communities. Parker Palmer, in a paper on the relationship between the churches and the renewal of public life, said that

> only as we are willing to [face in our own lives the contradictions of society] can God use us to bring the transcendent powers of love into the world. If we spend our lives retreating from the places where contradictions are found we will never become channels for the power of reconciling love.[17]

What are the *most pressing* issues facing members of your congregation? Take the risk of talking about them. In the process we can expect to be shaken at times, but the confrontation will not kill us. Boredom and superficiality are much more likely to kill, albeit slowly.

Let us risk talking to each other so that we may learn and live.

3. Pray For and Love Your Enemies

The Contras or the Sandinistas (choose one). The man who molests the child down the street. The Russians. The white-hooded Klu Klux Klansman who hurled a firebomb into my friend's backyard. The engineer at Kwajalein Missile Range. My rival at the office. Defense contractors. Stripminers. Real estate developers. My detractors who mean to do me harm. White supremacists in South Africa. My neighbor who supervises the operation of the nearby nuclear power plant that is repeatedly cited for safety violations. The pious church leader who is friendly to my face but cuts me up in ribbons behind my back. The person who unjustly accuses me. The teacher who discriminates against my son. The man who is spreading false rumors about my husband. The emergency medical technician whose error of judgment caused my friend's death. The farmer who fortifies his cattle's feed with hormones and additives that will end up on the dinner tables of the nation. The oil company that insists on drilling at Prudhoe Bay despite the environmental risk. The owners of the coal gasification project on Navajo tribal lands that is damaging the land and interfering with sheep grazing. The airline executive who knows his charter planes are metal-fatigued but flies them anyway. The carting company that illegally dumped medical refuse close to the sandy shores where children wade and build sand castles. The military officer who approved the use of Agent Orange in the Vietnam War. The men of South American military regimes who maintain their power by threats, mysterious disappearances of "dissidents," and torture chambers. The drunk driver who killed the high school senior. The system that withholds public health care to children of poverty. The system that allows greed to go unchallenged. The industrialist who prefers to use cheap labor in Mexico rather than labor union workers in Detroit. The politician who gains voters by false optimism rather than hard truth. The AIDS-infected man who passed the disease to the widow's only child.

According to Bonhoeffer, "By our enemies Jesus means those who are quite intractable and utterly unresponsive to our love, who forgive us nothing when we forgive them all, who requite love with hatred and our service with derision."[18]

Whoever your enemies are, pray for them and love them.

> To love our enemies in the nuclear era . . . will mean certain things to the Christian. Understanding is one form of love: the understanding of our enemies' history, culture, needs, prejudices, geographical constrictions, profound beliefs. Love also implies familiarity, personal encounters with those who hold such "enemy" beliefs. Love may not directly transform institutional hostilities into amicable relations, but love can and traditionally has informed and enriched human interactions from which institutional behavior derives. To that end . . . in both personal and public life, the Christian urgently but patiently must be a bearer of reconciling love in the world, daring to be at peace with others as God in Christ has made a full and reconciling peace with us.[19]

No one is beyond the saving grace of God. Prayer opens up channels to God's grace. Prayer changes the pray-er—that is, the person praying—and the person or persons prayed for. Prayer topples the mighty from their thrones and humanizes those in seats of power. Prayer was behind the civil rights movement; prayer will usher in a new order of justice in South Africa. Prayer for the enemies of

God's Creation can usher in God's new reign of love. "Love your enemies and pray for those who persecute you, so that you may become children of your father who is in heaven" (Matt. 5:44).

4. Revive and Renew Ritual and Reconnect It with Daily Life and Work

In this century humankind became caught in a bind, for in this century our ability to destroy has outrun our capability to control the means of aggression. As long as our tools and weapons were those we held in our hands, we could inflict harm and even kill, but we could also keep the lid on the violence that is a part of the human condition. But now weapons are out of our hands. They lie buried deep in missile silos somewhere under the remote Dakota prairie or embedded in the holds of a fast-attack submarine cruising somewhere beneath the waters of the globe. The weapons are out there, but exactly where I don't know. I can neither see, touch, nor feel them. I can only existentially feel the dread of their power that hangs over us all like the cold hand of death.

In this century we have also seen the decline of the authentic ritual that once linked together religion and reality. Sure, the forms of ritual are still there, but they have become disconnected from life. We tricked ourselves into thinking that we could keep the forms without the substance, but it turned out to be like one more diet Coke—the fuzz and flavor without the sugar and a hefty dose of caffeine. The laity gave over the realm of religious ritual to the clerics, who have forgotten—if indeed they ever knew—that the dance, the fiesta, the baseball game are rites located at the heart of life. And without the ritual—the liturgy—that which symbolizes and embodies our life and its meaning, we are pitifully empoverished.

Ritual, properly understood, is the liturgy that encompasses every aspect of life. Behind its masks and ceremonies and stunts is the true meaning, which is its penetration into cosmic reality and the core of existence. Life and death, past and future, sadness and joy, courage, individual striving for perfection, danger and evil encountered and overcome, transcending of self, harmony of body, emotions and spirit, music and humor, laughter and fun—all these aspects of reality are, or ought to be, captured in liturgical ritual. As Thomas Merton reminded us,

> liturgy, in the original and classical sense of the word, is a political activity. *Leitourgia* was a "public work," a contribution made by a free citizen of the *polis* to the celebration and manifestation of the visible life of the *polis*.[20]

In A.M. Hocart's opinion, "The object of ritual is to secure full life and to *escape from evil.*"[21] And according to Becker, "the invention and practice of ritual . . . is first and foremost a technique for promoting the good life and *averting evil*" (emphasis added.)[22]

By allowing the *essence* of real life and experience to be drained out of the *elements* of ritual, we are left adrift, devoid of a very basic means by which humankind historically has been able to both absorb and control evil.

Initially, the title of this commandment was *Recognize and Acknowledge Evil and Handle Aggression Constructively.* In it I was going to suggest that engaging in sports and games of mastery and competition and participating in spectator sports are all healthy and utterly necessary outlets for the evil and aggression that lurks just below the surface within each of us. But then I thought of how often and quickly large sporting events spill over into the mobilization of violence among fans and how many Yankee–Red Sox games erupt into fights in the bleachers and about the naked aggression unleashed in too many English football stadiums. So sports by themselves are inadequate outlets for aggression.

At the same time there is a link between the fiesta, sports, and religious ritual. Indeed as Robert Jay Lifton has pointed out, the Olympic Games have their origins as part of religious festivals.[23] Michael Novak describing the meaning of sports, on the one hand, and Octavio Paz illustrating the significance of festivals, on the other, are both tapping into the same phenomenon, which, they both concede, is akin to religious ritual. About being the player or spectator in sports, Novak says,

> the heart of human reality is courage, honesty, freedom, community, excellence: the heart is sports. . . . Within its formal ritual, hatred is permitted, even nourished. . . . Football is an almost revelatory liturgy. It externalizes the warfare in our hearts and offers us a means of knowing ourselves and wresting some grace from our true natures. . . . Sports are the highest products of civilization and the most accessible, lived, experiential sources of the civilized spirit. . . . Cease to play, cease civilization.[24]

In the fiesta, according to Paz,

> everything is united: good and evil, day and night, the sacred and the profane. Everything merges, loses shape and individuality and returns to the primordial mass. The fiesta is a cosmic experiment, an experiment in disorder, reuniting contradictory elements and principles in order to bring about renascence of life. Ritual promotes a rebirth; . . . renews the fertility of the mother or the earth. . . . The fiesta is a return to a remote and undifferented state. . . . The group emerges purified and strengthened from the plunge into chaos. . . . Lay or religious, orgy or saturnalia, the fiesta is a social act based on full participation. Life and death, joy and sorrow, music and noise are united.[25]

The fiesta, the game, and religious ritual ought to be brought together again, for the very word *liturgy* has roots in a social reality larger than the way we have interpreted it. Liturgy, derived from two Greek words, *laos* (people) and *ergon* (work), is the work of the people. In its original context, liturgy comes from the realm of public service, public works, municipal responsibility—the building and maintaining of roads, civic buildings, and docks—public service for community well-being. Liturgy can, once again, become genuine public service and private consolation also, as it unites the divergent strands of human variety, emotion, intellect, and body into satisfying expression. A revived, enriched, and renewed liturgy would help us to be at one with ourselves and with each other, with God and the whole totality of the created order.

Without the texture of our daily lives (including its pain and evil), without the links with every aspect of our ordinary experience, our liturgies are just so many hollow words and dead actions signifying nothing. Unless we can be more successful in connecting our liturgies with our lives, all of the liturgical reform of the last several decades will have been for naught.

Liturgy will come to life and express life to the extent that the world comes to the liturgy, it will come to life to the degree that it expresses the tempo, the heartbeat, the sweat, tears, and the hope of humanity. John Robinson has said that liturgy is "the great work-shop of the new world."[26]

Let us revive and renew ritual and reconnect it with daily life and work.

5. Learn from Others

Following the final meeting of the Commission on World Mission, in Santa Domingo, the members were passing the time. It was a balmy February evening in the Caribbean. We'd finished out business and were not up to much else save "shooting the breeze" for a few hours. As we sat there, my mind wandered, and I thought about my fellow members. I studied their faces, I looked into their eyes and listend to their voices. Most of them were middle-aged; two were close to retirement—so they had had a lot of living behind them. I wondered how they had gotten their start, what had been the formative influences of their lives that had brought them both to the commission and, most especially, to their careers of leadership and service in the church and the community.

We talked about it for awhile. It is a small commission with less than a dozen members, divided among lay people, bishops, and priests. So we knew each other reasonably well, and the conversation was easy. Astonishingly, almost half of the members had been a part of the Episcopal Church's College Work Program of the early 1960s, which sent college and seminary students to work in such urban areas as Jersey City, New York's Lower East Side, the Mission District of San Francisco, and among migrant workers in upstate New York and in the Southwest, in Mexican villages, on Dakota Indian reservations, in Alaska, and into the Arctic Circle. Most of the others got their start as exchange students and through student travels in other lands. In every case, the members had been influenced by other cultures in their late teen years or early twenties, and in every case those early experiences had cast a long shadow over the rest of their lives.

To cite a few who were with us that lazy evening: there was a North Carolina doctor—Rambo by name, but he is nothing like Rambo, the cult hero—who worked as a doctor in Uganda just before the dangerous days of Idi Amin; there was the director of a seminary in the Dominican Republic, responsible for the training of indigenous ordained leaders, who worked with migrant laborers in upstate New York; an Ecuadorian bishop, an Inca Indian, who started out as a lawyer and young Roman Catholic priest in several Central and South American countries; a Chinese-Mexican who runs a family Chinese restaurant and had been a student in Texas; the head of a national missionary society who got his start on a summer project in Alaska; an American bishop who was a young missionary bishop in Botswana; another American bishop who started as a missionary in Costa Rica; a lay woman from Hawaii who is director of an immigrant service center; and another lay member who learned his lessons on an Iowa farm.

Twenty-five years old and 120,000 volunteers later, the Peace Corps remains one of the best and most enduring ways to learn those lessons in mortal restlessness that will be lifelong and life-giving. And as with the student college work projects of the 1950s and 1960s, most who have been Peace Corps volunteers would agree that they received much more than they ever gave. A group of Yale students who had been Peace Corps volunteers sounded like younger versions of Commission on World Mission members. On the occasion of the Peace Corps' twenty-fifth birthday, a few of them were interviewed.

Allen Turner, who went to an uplands farming project in the Dominican Republic, said, "It was an amazing revelation when you climb into another culture . . . with people different from Americans you grow."[27] Turner now works in agriculture, the line of work "I'd never dreamed I'd be doing [had it not been for the Peace Corps]."[28] Overcoming cultural barriers, learning the language, struggling with fleas, dysentery, grass huts without furniture, maleria, tapeworms, the shattering of naivete, learning unpleasant truths about American neocolonialism, becoming disillusioned with American consumption and complacency, often with neither adequate food nor water—against the backdrop of these experiences, the volunteers are changed. Stephen Bingham, who went to Sierra Leone, said that "it's a humbling experience for those of us who live in a microwave society" and one that is staying with him, for as he remarked, "The Peace Corps has been a critical element in my maintaining a commitment to social change. There's an ongoing hum in the back of my mind that there are people starving out there."[29]

In many cases, the Peace Corps influenced the volunteers' later choice of career, like Allen Turner, who never thought he would be in agriculture, and Nick Allis, Zygmunt Broel-Plater, and Whitney Sanders. Nick Allis, who went to Nigeria to teach school in the mid-1960s, is now a public-interest lawyer. Zyg Broel-Plater, who went to Ethiopia and also became a lawyer, feels the Peace Corps "teaches you what you can do as a human being."[30] Broel-Plater, now a law professor at Boston College, says he is trying to pass on to his students what he learned: "You're here to make a life as well as a living, and if you're lucky, a difference."[31] Living in Third World countries understandably tarnished the volunteers' image of the United States. But, according to Whitney Sanders, who went to Sierra Leone and returned to pursue a career in urban housing, "I learned about making do with what you're given, through channels that are not often used, and against pressures you don't often feel . . . making do with materials that are less costly, and coming up with new ways to interpret common problems in building methods."[32]

This is not intended as a plug for the Peace Corps (although it certainly deserves one), but rather I'm using the Peace Corps as an illustration of what can happen during the formative years of life (or in any years, for that matter) if people are set in a different environment where they have to learn from the cultures in order to get by. Samuel Gejdenson, who represents my district in the U.S. House of Representatives, told me that he is persuaded that every member of the House and Senate should be required to travel to Third World nations because the reality of other peoples' lives and worldviews (about which Congress passes legislation) can only be *experienced*, not merely read about in congressional reports and studies. Gejdenson himself has been deeply affected by just one trip to El Salvador. Volumes have been written, and opinions are rife, about the different ways people learn, but there is very little disagreement that *people learn best from experience*. Everyone needs to drink deeply from the wells of other experiences, other cultures, other life-styles.

As far as religious traditions go, we have a great deal to learn from the Mennonites, Hutterites, and Quakers—lessons about sharing, pacificism, communal living, and public service. Granny Dodge, the wise old Maine woman I began this book with, has the wisdom of a past age to pass on. Let us talk with all the Granny Dodges and all our grandparents while there is yet time.

Let us learn from Native Americans. The half million or so Native Americans who have moved to urban areas, and also many left on the reservation, are in need of learning the lessons of their culture just as we are beginning to realize what Native Americans can teach every American. A Rhode Island cleric, after his first visit to the Indian lands of South Dakota and the native way, said,

> It is certain that there are different values for the Indian society and our society. Their emphasis is much more on the group and the tribe where we tend to emphasize our individual accomplishments. They also have a different sense of time than we do. Time is always with them. They seem to have a spiritual quality of accepting time as endless with no immediate sense of urgency. While, of course, for most of us we want to use every second, and to be sure to plan for the future. Where in our society youth is venerated; in their society old age is venerated. They face the world with a sense of cooperation, particularly with nature. All of life is a religious way of life in which the whole universe is unified. This contrasts to much of our thinking which is highly competitive, where we must conquer nature and do not care about the environment at all.[33]

We need to do everything possible to encourage cultural exchange. Sister-cities projects link American cities with foreign counterparts where citizens exchange visits and ideas and work together on common projects. Organizations such as International Physicians for the Prevention of Nuclear War sponsor exchange visits between American and Soviet doctors; there are farmer exchange visits and student exchanges. Habitat for Humanity builds houses in Third World countries (as well as right here in the U.S.) where local people work alongside American volunteers. Also the Mennonites and the Quakers both have voluntary service programs similar to the Peace Corps—and they're open to Christians of other traditions. In short, the rich variety of cross-cultural programs are legion. They offer us hope and opportunity.

Churches are uniquely suited for setting up the conditions for cross-cultural learning. The largest share of every parish's youth budget ought to go toward funding cross-cultural projects, and every denominational headquarters knows of missionary areas that would gladly welcome young American workers for the summer or even a semester. In the case of selecting candidates for the ordained ministry, churches have a particular opportunity because they are able to prescribe the type of experience they expect candidates to bring with them. Many denominations require that their candidates for ordination take a course in clinical pastoral education (chaplaincy intern programs in general and psychiatric hospitals and the like, where students learn about themselves and others). In the same manner, denominations could require service in a missionary or cross-cultural experience as a condition of acceptance. Furthermore, denominational commissions on ministry could begin recruiting people for the ordained ministry who have recently returned from Peace Corps, VISTA, Habitat for Humanity, Greenpeace, and other such projects.

A church that seeks and requires of its leaders cross-cultural experience is going to be a very different church than the one we experience today—a much better, broader, and more human church.

Let us learn from others that we may live.

6. Act

When all is said and done, the ministry of words is as easy as it is cheap. Our liturgies have become lifeless and our rituals impotent because we have failed to communicate the *essence* of the gospel with the *substance* of our lives. Furthermore, our evangelistic campaigns have failed and are doomed to continued failure because of the shallowness of our actions as Christian communities.

Anti-apartheid Christians in South Africa have described the predicament of the church that fails to act. According to David Bosch, a Dutch Reformed theologian,

> The stumbling block often happens to be the church herself—the very church whose raison d'etre is precisely to be a pointer to Christ and attract others to him. The church too often fulfills the role of a social agency for the relief of painful disappointments where uncomfortable memories and awkward expectations are being covered up. The church has become the cozy ghetto of kindred souls, the cave into which we flee when day-to-day problems are too much for us.[34]

And *The Kairos Document,* also out of South Africa, states that "much of what we do in our Church services has lost its relevance. . . . Our services and sacraments have been appropriated to serve the need of the individual for comfort and security.[35]

The North American Christian looks longingly on the vitality of the South African anti-apartheid church and African Christianity in general, as well as that of the Latin American church. Ardent Christians who have means and opportunity visit Brazilian base communities and African villages and are often changed forever by the experience of seeing four hundred Christians baptized in an afternoon or being present in a stadium full of people for the funeral of a child gunned down by the police in a South African township. Bishop Tutu and Allen Boesak are our heros, and we are moved by the life and death of El Salvador's assassinated Archbishop Oscar Romero. We look wistfully at these devoted and courageous Christians and the thousands just like them who also make a costly witness. But we fail to translate their situation into ours. In fact, the reasons for the vitality of the church in locations of oppressive political regimes is that, generally speaking, the church is engaged in the culture of the people; it is on the side of the people as they seek a more just society. There the church is not remaining neutral; it is taking positions; it is taking sides; it is acting. To be sure, one might say that the issues and the injustice are more obvious in the extreme cruelty of a South Africa or in the military dictatorships of Latin America where the great majority of the people are poor. But what we fail to realize is that the issues confronting American society and the American earth are just as dangerous; it is just that they are different. If members of Nicaraguan base communities could lead in the successful struggle against the tyrannical Somoza, if faithful Catholics could lend the energy to the struggle to rid the Philippines of Ferdinand Marcos, if South African anti-apartheid Christians—both black and white—can force justice in their country, as they are on the verge of doing right now, there is no reason why American Christians cannot name the damaging issues of our culture and act on them accordingly.

Or do we understand but fail to act because we know the cost of action and are unwilling to pay the price of sacrifice?

Or, is it seduction, as Jim Wallis, a founder of Sojourners Community, has suggested? Are we seduced into thinking that the dilemmas of our culture, of Creation, and of the church really aren't so bad; that, after all, I'm OK and you're OK? In Wallis's words,

> in the United States our chief enemy is not persecution [as in areas of the world already alluded to]. It is seduction. We are a people seduced by a way of thinking, a way of living, that is irreconcilable with the lordship of Christ.[36]

But whether it is the American church's failure to make the connection between faith and culture or our lack of willingness to pay the price of acting in culture and Creation or that we are seduced, the consequences of our inaction, both for individual citizens and for Christian communities, are painfully evident.

Every citizen has an obligation to take an active part in the public affairs of the nation beyond the obligatory participation in job and family. Just having the right beliefs will not do. It is our actions that speak. Richard Steele, one of South Africa's first religious conscious objectors, wrote the following during his imprisonment:

> I have learned that it is not enough to espouse a position or point of

view merely verbally (even though it may be a good one) and expect it to be listened to and accepted at face value. For it to be credible and influential the point of view must be personally embodied, given practical lifestyle support. *It is the day to day living out of our beliefs which carry weight and have moral authority.* [emphasis added].[37]

A number of years ago a New Haven United Church of Christ pastor, Arthur Bradley, helped me to see my responsibility in the community. We were both graduate students at the same New York City university and frequently traveled on the same train between New York and New Haven. Art, aside from being a graduate student and busy pastor, was very active in the New Haven community, and I will never forget the time he asked me what I did in the community. I felt his question impertinent. After all, I answered him, wasn't I parent of three active school children and wife of a busy professor? Wasn't I fully occupied teaching at the local branch of the state university, and wasn't I trying to finish a Ph.D. dissertation, plus participating in my parish? Isn't that more than enough activity for one human being to handle? I asked. And look, this situation is only temporary, just while I'm going to school. "But what do you do to contribute to the public good?" Art pressed. What about the growing number of poor people seeking permanent homes? What was I doing about that problem? How about the quality of public education? Wasn't I participating in local politics or the party caucus? Art really put me on the spot, for I honestly had to admit that I hadn't given my personal involvement in public affairs much thought. Art's questions both embarrassed and chastened me. I should hasten to add that he wasn't suggesting that I take on one more activity, as such, but rather that I rearrange my commitments so as to allow some service in the community. Needless to say, I took Art's lesson to heart.

But that was well over a decade ago, during which time every denomination has spent time and money to enhance the ministry of the laity. And, it must be conceded, every denomination has—in large measure—failed. They have not succeeded in getting across the idea of lay responsibility in and for the world. Prior to the 1987 synod in Rome titled "The Vocation and Mission of the Laity in the World," U.S. Roman Catholic bishops conducted a consultation on the status of lay participation in the world. Summarizing the results of the survey, Robert Kinast concluded that the "impetus for most active Catholic lay people in the United States will remain church-centered" and that there is still "too much attention given to church ministries at the expense of wider areas of responsibility in the family, neighborhood, work, civic groups, political-social-economic life."[38] The words of "A Chicago Declaration of Christian Concern," written in 1977, bear repeating: "In the last analysis, the Church speaks to and acts upon the world through her laity. Without a dynamic laity, conscious of its personal ministry to the world, the Church, in effect, does not speak or act.[39]

But clergy are not to be excepted, they are not to be considered a special class apart from everybody else, for everyone needs to remember that Christ came for the sake of the world—not the church—and Christ lived and died for the well-being of the world and of every person and aspect of Creation. We can no longer afford to leave the issues of peace, justice, and ecology to hippies, peaceniks, a handful of Roman Catholic bishops, and the Sierra Club. According to Arthur Laffin, "At this critical moment in history, people of faith and conscience face a moral imperative to translate their beliefs into nonviolent action for life."[40]

Everyone does not have to do everything, but no one should do nothing in the public sector. What a difference it would make if everyone would take *just one* public problem, issue, or interest and work with it: running for the school board; starting an affordable, nonprofit housing corporation; joining the town Democratic or Republican committee or the League of Women Voters and using these groups as the forum for studying public problems and for promoting political candidates who espouse responsible positions; organizing candidate forums for the debate of election issues; running for public office; following local environmental issues and making an issue of them; taking part in public prayer vigils outside nuclear weapons plants, as well as engaging in nonviolent civil disobedience and fasts in certain circumstances to illustrate the meaning of divine obedience. This is not volunteerism. It is not do-goodism in the traditional sense, for no amount of volunteer activity can take the place of political and legislative action. This is the exercise of public responsibility. This is the shouldering of public responsibility to make our government and public institutions work for justice, the welfare of all citizens, and the well-being of our earth. We can and we must use the structures we have already as channels of reform and renewal.

Start close to home. What is just one problem in your community or even your neighborhood that needs attention? Start there, taking encouragement from the words of the *Tao Teh Ching:* "A journey of a thousand miles starts from where your feet are."[41]

Look at a few examples of just what one person can do. *One doctor* (Edward McDermott) investigated and discovered that cyanide, ethyl benzenene, mythylene chloride, chloroform, and ammonia are being dumped in the river by a local pharmaceutical plant and involved one hundred more doctors on his hospital staff to bring the problem to public awareness and action. *One woman*

(Desire Parker) forewent a profit of $2.3 million to donate her 234 acre tract of land to a public trust that will keep it a wilderness area (and she is not a wealthy woman, having worked at an ordinary job all her life). *One farm labor leader* (Cesar Chavez) organized his fellow Mexican-American vegetable and fruit pickers to form a farm workers union in 1972. *One small group* of Micronesian women of the tiny Micronesian nation of Palau are leading the fight to keep the antinuclear clause in Palau's constitution (despite the promise of millions of dollars worth of funding and strong pressure from the United States, which regards Palau as a fallback site in case it loses its military bases in the Philippines in 1991). *One Irish rock music star* (Bob Geldof) took the plight of Ethiopia's starving to heart and initiated the Live Aid concert, which raised $70 million for the cause. *One retired Methodist minister* (George Hill) wrote and edited *The Hill Newsletter*—a compilation of articles, book reviews, quotes, and sermons on peacemaking—sent it to friends and colleagues to raise their consciousness. *One successful Hartford real estate developer* (Bill Farley) also started a newsletter—*Between Sundays*—this one about ministry and ethics in business. *One New York City business executive* (Eugene Lang) offered to pay the college tuition for all the sixth graders at the Harlem elementary school from which he himself had graduated decades before. This one individual decided he was going to marshal his resources to do his part in breaking the cycle of poverty and lack of opportunity for just one class of children. Because of one man, there are now 125 similar programs in twenty-four cities throughout the land.[42] The annals of history overflow with laws, reforms, and movements that began when *one* ordinary person decided to act.

"My children, our love should not be just words and talk; it must be true love that shows itself in *action* (1 John 3:18). Let us act in God's Creation that we may live.

7. Unite Personal Morality with the Common Good

If we believe that Creation is a seamless fabric connecting all of life, we acknowledge an intimate connection between the using and abusing of the universe and the using and abusing of people and personal relationships. There is an intimate connection between the way my household lives in the intimacy of the family and the way we live as public citizens. A rip at any point in the fabric affects the whole piece. It is more than a mere broken link in a chain, for a weak link affects not only the link itself but the whole chain as well. The responsibility I exercise—or fail to exercise—in my household among the family is as important as the responsibility I am called to exercise in the wider community. (And it is also more likely to be immediately fruitful because I can more readily influence family members with whom I share my day-to-day life than members of the public.) Personal morality and the common good are—or ought to be—apiece. Jim Wallis has reminded us that

> we are tragically nearsighted is we fail to see the spiritual connections between our abandonment of the poor, despoiling of the earth, cultural acceptance of racial and sexual exploitation, approval of abortion on demand, and willingness to commit genocide against enemy populations.[43]

A good marriage is like a fire burning on a dark January evening that warms the hearts of the beloved partners as well as those of others around and beyond the hearth of love. A good marriage is like a tall, leafy oak tree providing shade in the heat of the day. "Many waters cannot quench love, neither can floods drown it" (Song of Solomon 8:7a). The love of a wholesome marriage erupts and spills over into every aspect of life just as the fresh spring rain nurtures fertility, new life, and new beginnings.

A good marriage is life's greatest gift and life's greatest blessing. A good marriage is life-giving (literally), life-sustaining, and life looking forward. The fruit of a good marriage is its gift to the future; it is children who are blessing in the present and hope in the future.

But every statistic also tells us how very rare a good marriage is, how psychologically and physically damaged and abused partners and their children can become in a marriage. Surely God weeps over those marriages that anticipate heaven but are lived in hell. And it is very easy to understand why marriages fail, why dreams so quickly degenerate into nightmares. When we feel impotent about changing our world, the futility of so many of our actions, the deep uncertainty as to whether humankind will survive into the next century, the anxiety—the awful dread of our times—beckons us to hit out. As we administer the blow, we strike what is most available to be hit: the husband or wife, the children who—as often as not—only represent more demands and more mouths to feed. The stress builds up, the demands and uncertainty of contemporary life, the conflict over unmet expectations, the rent, the mortgage to pay. So we administer the blow. A few blows, a marriage and family can sustain, but all too quickly comes the knockout punch that ends the fight and sends the players to their separate corners alone and bleeding, there to lick their wounds in solitude. And surely God weeps over those who have never been able to form a sustaining and loving relationship. Surely God knows their loneliness and feels deeply for them.

The church is a human institution; it is made up of fallible human beings, human beings who have been and are just as affected by the poison that enters personal relationships as anyone else in society. Many of the clergy who regularly officiate over the exchange of marriage vows, who guide the partners as they pledge themselves "for better, for worse; for richer, for poorer; in sickness and in health; to love and to cherish until parted by death" have themselves broken the same vows they are commanding the couple before them to keep. They realize the duplicity. They realize the incongruity of expecting the couple to do that which they themselves have been unable to accomplish. Of the professional staff numbering ten of a leading Methodist church in a large university town in Texas, nine members have been divorced. This scenario is repeated in just about every major city across the nation among churches of every mainline denomination. Is not this instability something we should worry about? Of course. And many in the church are rethinking marriage, divorce, and other relationships.

Should we have rites of betrothal so the couple can test their relationship in advance of marriage? Should there be services of blessing for same-sex unions? How about postmarital unions? John Spong, the Episcopal bishop of Newark, believes there should be. A question is, Should the church maintain the ideal of the "traditional marriage," which is so illusive to so many members of society? And is it fair or realistic for the church to withold the liturgical blessing of gay and lesbian relationships? If homosexuality is a matter of nature—as many believe—about which the person has no choice, isn't the church being cruel, unfair, and judgmental to withold the blessing of such relationships? Or how about ordination for the same reason? Should persons be denied the rites and privileges of the church because of the way they were born and about which they can do nothing (if, in fact, they wanted to)? These are critical matters, and feelings and opinion run high on both the yea and nay sides.

Looking at the issue of the ordination of homosexual persons in particular, Alexander Stewart said in his report on the 1988 Lambeth Conference—the once-a-decade worldwide conference of Anglican bishops—that it was not the issue of the ordination of women, especially the ordination of women as bishops, that threatened to break up the Anglican Communion but rather issues of sexuality. According to Stewart,

> While sitting with a group of African bishops, one heard the comment, "We would more likely leave the Anglican Communion on the issue of sexuality than on the ordination of women." When asked why, he answered, "Deep down we do not really think the ordination of women is wrong, it is just nowhere near ready for us at this time . . . we see it as a 'justice issue' whereas we view the sexuality issue as a biblical/moral

issue on which there can be no change. Had the Conference voted to take the liberal position, it would have been very hard for us to stay within the Communion. It would have been a 'break', not an 'impairment'."[44]

No doubt these issues will occupy Christians for many years to come. In fact, according to Philip Turner,

> the battle for the soul of the Episcopal Church, which is also the battle over the ethics of sex, is simply this. Shall the soul of the Episcopal Church become a "trimmer" who sets her sail to suit the prevailing wind or shall it be the soul of a church with the requisite love and courage to offer through her teaching and example of the lives of her members an alternative to a society which seems increasingly incapable of anything more than "limited engagements?"[45]

The battle has only just begun, but as it heats up it is likely to forge new political alignments among church members as well as to rupture some old ones. For example, for many who are promoting gay and lesbian rights, this is the first time they have become active in political issues. They are using many of the methods that have been bread and butter to liberals and radicals, that is, public meetings, protests, demonstrations, and confrontations. Many people who had never considered participating in a demonstration outside a racially segregated business or a nuclear armaments plant are getting active in gay and lesbian issues. The awakening of political consciousness has been energizing; it has served to encourage and unify a constituency, in both church and society, which heretofore has been largely invisible, ignored, and discriminated against. On the other hand, the liberal and radical camps are divided. Some side with gays and lesbians and their supporters. But many people, who have had a lifetime of taking liberal and radical positions on public issues, for the first time in their experience are finding themselves far to the right on sexual morality issues. These people would readily identify *both* with Cesar Chavez or Jesse Jackson or Bishop Tutu on social issues as well as with Jerry Falwell and fundamentalist Christian denominations on sexual matters. And these people, who are politically liberal and conservative on moral issues, are caught. To date, most of them have remained silent on their real misgivings concerning sexual matters, which they see as issues of morality and biblical tradition, not justice. They do not know how to deal with their conservativism in one area of their thought and with liberalism in another. For them it is a new dilemma. In part it's a reluctance to tarnish the luster of their liberal position, but also it is the case that they feel genuinely isolated and uncertain. They recoil at any suggestion that they might be taken as being judgmental. And after being considered judgmental, the next worst thing the liberal hates is to appear as unjust. So this group feels caught.

Nonetheless, those who are timid about speaking the unpopular word are going to have to gain the confidence to come forward. A great deal is at stake, for if we are no longer to expect our church leaders to model in their own lives healthy, wholesome personal relationships as an example in a fractured world, the church is in deep trouble. If we are going to drop the ideal of the strong, healthy family as the basic social unit (hard as that ideal may be to live up to); if we are going to abandon the notion that the family is a microcosm of just, loving, and cordial relations among members that we expect to replicate in the larger society; then we fail to serve both the church and the larger society responsibly.

Whatever the outcome of the struggle, the eyes of society will follow the church's debate keenly. And as church members continue to talk, it is appropriate that we remind ourselves that the early Christians were easily identifiable by the quality of their lives. Tertullian (circa A.D. 160–225), one of the early church fathers, once quoted a pagan as saying, "See how Christians love one another." As we talk, it is imperative that we continue to love one another and ever seek to unite personal morality with the common good. It matters greatly that we are consistent in our personal lives and in our public lives, for we are known primarily by what we do and how we act. We are intended to be light to the world and leaven in the lump; we are intended to make a difference and to show forth that difference in the quality of our lives. God's Creation is a seamless fabric, it is a whole piece. We have a moral responsibility to keep the fabric whole and, where it is worn or torn, to repair it. Personal morality must never be divorced from the common good; the two must never be broken asunder, for as *The Kairos Document* soberly reminds us,

> the people look to the Church, especially in the midst of our present crisis, for moral guidance. In order to provide this the Church must first make its stand absolutely clear and never tire of explaining and dialoguing about it. . . . There must be no misunderstanding about the moral duty.[46]

Let us unite personal morality with the common good that as a church united we may bind up the sores of a society so disunited and in unity show to all the world our love for each other and for every aspect of God's Creation.

8. Sacrifice

There is no way around the sacrifice required if we are truly to care for and to heal God's Creation. Some have already paid for their commitment with the sacrifice of their lives—like Dietrich Bonhoeffer, Martin Luther King, Oscar Romero. The pages of church history are drenched in the blood of martyrs; indeed, the church is founded on the lives of prophets and martyrs.

There are others right now, still living, who are showing us the meaning of sacrifice: Roman Catholic Archbishop Raymond Hunthausen of Seattle, an outspoken peace activist who has withheld the portion of his taxes that would go to the support of the armaments industry; Archbishop Helder Camara, a central figure in the struggle for justice in Brazil, who was officially silenced by the Brazilian press (so was not heard on radio or seen on television) from 1968–78; Cesar Chavez, president of the United Farm Workers, who recently fasted to call attention to the pesticides causing illness—especially cancer—in field workers who harvest table grapes; Allen Boesak, an outspoken leader in the efforts to end apartheid in South Africa, who regularly receives death threats.

The sacrifice some of us make will lead us to death. For others, sacrifice will mean imprisonment as conscious objectors. It will mean death threats for some and drastically altered ways of living. Take Arthur Laffin, for example. Art would probably succeed in any business he put his mind to (he has already authored two books), but he works as a house painter—a job that involves short projects that permit Art to be available for his real ministry, which is being a peace worker. Most of the time Art is participating in peace vigils and demonstrations at various armaments factories or military installations. He is frequently in court and more frequently being arrested for participating in nonviolent demonstrations of civil disobedience. He travels around the country to many locations where nuclear weapons are manufactured and deployed. He spent six months in jail for his part in trying to disarm a Trident submarine in Connecticut. During Holy Week, Art leads a week-long peace pilgrimage from New Haven to Groton, staying in church halls and talking to people along the route about peace and the need for disarmament. The pilgrimage ends outside a nuclear submarine boatyard where he participates in the Good Friday Stations of the Cross. Art does it every year, with a host of others. One year, just as Art was apprehended for attempting to carry the message of peace inside the gates of the boatyard, he explained his actions to the press. He told them, "We're called to be light in the darkness, water in the desert, healing through blood, power through non-violence."[47] Some of us are called to make sacrifices such as Art's. Everyone, if they are lucky, knows someone like Art Laffin who serves as a loving example of sacrifice and who by actions (not words) stirs our consciences to try to do likewise.

All of us, if we wish to be faithful, will have to make some sacrifices. Indeed, if our faith is real it should make us willing to both heal the environment and improve the lot of those who have too little of the world's goods. Think of it this way. If it were a matter of life and death for one of our children, or one of our brothers or sisters, wouldn't we make any sacrifice that would be required to bring the suffering one back to health or safety? So let us consider our fellow citizens of this planet as our children and as our brothers and sisters. And let us ask ourselves how much of the material goods we have at our disposal do we really need? How much of what we have could be sacrificed if it were a matter of life or death to a member of our family? For however indirectly it may be, the ways we live and conduct our affairs and our patterns of possession and consumption *are* matters of life and death to our children and our brothers and sisters with whom we share this planet. Being willing to sacrifice does not mean that everyone has to sacrifice everything, and sacrifice will be interpreted differently across the board, but *some sacrifice* is a moral obligation. For Carl Mitchum, it is sacrificing sophisticated toys and gadgets with which our lives are cluttered:

> My suggestion is that now, in our highly technological culture, there is a need for some Christians freely to give up major aspects of technology as an eschatological witness just like [in an earlier age] St. Francis of Assisi undertook a radical giving up of wealth as a witness to the Kingdom.[48]

Day-to-day sacrifices will need to become habits of our lives, habits of the heart, ways that become built into our daily actions. According to Jeremy Rifkin,

> It mean[s] that we need continually to ask ourselves how much is enough, and willing to discipline our appetites so that they remain within the bonds dictated by a sense of fair regard for every other living thing. It means that each time we consider a course of action, we ask ourselves how our decision will affect the wellbeing of the rest of the living kingdom today as well as that of future generations.[49]

The Christian ought to understand sacrifice, for our faith teaches us the meaning of offering ourselves as "a living sacrifice to God, dedicated to God's service" (Rom. 12:1). As Christians, our supreme example and model for sacrifice is the one who taught us—and still teaches us today—by the sacrifice of his death the profound meaning of sacrifice, that is, our Saviour Jesus Christ. Commenting on the events of Good Friday, Leonardo Boff says,

> Jesus must sacrifice everything. He holds nothing of himself back. Here on the threshold of death, even more intensely than during his lifetime he is a being for others. He surrenders everything, even the most intimate and private recesses of his being, in order to ransom all.[50]

Let us make the sacrifice. Let us offer ourselves as a living sacrifice so that our children and our brothers and sisters may live.

9. *Regard Service to Creation as Profoundly Religious*

While an ethic of responsibility is evident throughout the Scriptures of our faith, by church tradition and practice we must admit that Christians are ill equipped for the daunting task of responsibly caring for Creation.

The major stumbling block is Christians' conception of what is religious, of what constitutes spirituality and the spiritual journey. According to *The Kairos Document,*

> the answer [to Christians' lack of engagement in the world] must be sought in the *type of faith and spirituality* that has dominated Church life for centuries. As we all know, spirituality has tended to be an other-worldly affair that has very little, if anything at all, to do with the affairs of the world. Social and political matters were seen as worldly affairs that have nothing to do with the spiritual concerns of the Church. Moreover, spirituality has also been understood to be purely private and individualistic. Public affairs and social problems were thought to be beyond the sphere of spirituality.[51]

And as I myself have said elsewhere, the traditional spiritual journey has been interpreted by North American and northern Europeans as "my journey," "my interior life," "my spiritual direction," directed toward individual rather than broadly humanitarian and ecological values with the goal of personal perfection. "It is frequently characterized by insensitivity to the needs of concrete persons who surround Christians as they follow the spiritual way."[52] We have gone astray. The essence of religion is not to be found by turning away from the world; it is not in the standards of membership; not the mumbling of ancient creeds whose words have long since lost their meaning; it is not the solitary examination of my inner life or even poring over the fine points of Scripture. Religion is not the quiet hush in a sacred building or an ancient cathedral; it is not the bowing to metal icons and wooden crosses (ignoring the bloodied faces of the masses of humanity who are the real icons of Christ). Nobody said hush to Jesus when he kicked over the Temple tables and sent the coins jangling down the steps. The heart of religion is its penetration into the cosmic reality of all life; it is its identification with every aspect of the created order; it is saying with God from the depth of our being, "*It is good.*"

What is needed is a turnabout, a conversion, a revolution in what and who we regard as religious and where the aims of religion are best served.

We are, thank God, becoming attuned to looking at the hungry street person huddled over a steam grate on a New York City sidewalk in the depth of winter and understanding that there in the rags and misery is the great sacrament of God. In the same spirit we must look at the festering hazardous chemical waste dump or the ugly scars on the western landscape left by careless stripmining or at Johnston Island in the Pacific—nerve gas capital of the world—or at North Dakota farmlands that have turned to dust—and yes, see there God's suffering and there see God beckoning us to work for transformation. These places and the countless millions like them are monuments to humankind's greed and destructiveness and *also* locations where God through us—God's children—needs to be active in rectifying. The pained eyes through which we comprehend God's suffering children must be trained to look on God's groaning Creation. The pity, the sympathy, that pushes us to bind up the sores of the suffering people must be extended to bind up the wounds of suffering Creation. To quote *The Kairos Document* again,

> The Bible does not separate the human person from the world in which he or she lives; it does not separate the individual from the social or one's private life from one's public life. God redeems the whole person as part of his *whole creation* (Rom. 8:8–24).[53]

What is required is nothing less than "a truly biblical spirituality [that] would penetrate every aspect of human existence and would exclude *nothing* from God's redemptive will."[54]

Such a spirituality naturally urges us to take a fresh look at vocation. It is time to consider that perhaps Christians' *highest calling*, Christians' most devoted service, may not be to serve as the clergy of the church or as unordained church professionals or even to serve in such other traditional "people professions" as social work, nursing, teaching, and the like. It is time to consider that the *most religious* response to the gracious call of God may be to serve where the fabric of Creation most needs repair, reform, and renewal. We need agricultural scientists to develop grain that will flourish in extreme heat with little water. We need farmers to plant millions of trees all over the world and develop agriculture. We need chemists and biologists to analyze the effects of pollution on the land, in ocean waters, and in the atmosphere and to come up with concrete proposals and plans for improvement. We need a whole range of energy researchers to work in photovoltaics (electricity from the sun), to develop windmills, who will look into fuel cells (combining hydrogen and oxygen to make water and electricity), energy from tides and rivers. We need people who will work to develop alternatives to plastics, for plastics are like diamonds—they last forever. We need people who will devise safe methods of toxic waste disposal. We need environmentally responsible business executives and entrepreneurs who will illustrate that recycling and composting can be economically feasible. We need engineers and technicians who will further increase the gasoline mileage of automobiles. We need transportation planners to develop the nation's railroads and bus routes, people who will wean Americans from their love affair with the car and make public transportation workable. We need international bankers and economists who understand domestic and foreign money systems who will offer solutions to domestic and foreign debt. We need Christians who will regard service in these areas as *Christian vocation.* And we need to consider that the most respected Christian vocation might not be a missionary in a poverty-stricken nation or a highly ranked denominational official or even a Mother Teresa. We need to consider that the most devoted Christian servants may be politicans who run for political office—in the town, the city, the state, in the nation—who will run and get elected with the aim of making policies and shaping public opinion that will be good and responsible for all of God's creatures and for all of God's Creation. Finally, we need investigative news reporters who will call us to account for the times when we fall short in exercising our public responsibilities, reporters who will uncover the corruption of our institutions and remind us of the ideal of ethical practice.

Why? Because the issues of God's Creation are profoundly religious matters. Service to and in God's Creation is Christian calling of the highest order, and it is the most ardent form of religious devotion.

10. Watch and Give Thanks

It was a daytime flight just like so many others made by Balbir Mathur during the course of his travels as a consultant helping international businesses set up joint ventures. But this flight was different, not because the earth below was any different but because Mathur saw it in a different way.

> I was flying over Cyprus when it happened. I looked down, and it looked so small. And suddenly I could see how small the earth would look from a divine eye. And I was going round and round that little speck of dust. One side of the speck of dust was so different from the other. On one side there was plenty. And on the other side one child dies of malnutrition every few seconds and another is blinded or retarded.[55]

From that day forward, according to Mathur, "I decided to dedicate my life to fighting world hunger."[56] Through his efforts, 900,000 fruit-bearing trees have been planted in Mathur's native India since 1983. Fruit-bearing trees were a particularly good choice because they not only offset the greenhouse effect (like all trees, they absorb atmospheric carbon dioxide produced by industrial pollution) but they provide much needed food while at the same time countering deforestation.

Mathur's organization, Trees for Life, is one of about a half-dozen American groups whose goal is to feed the hungry and replenish the earth.

Balbir Mathur is a sign of hope, and he is correct in saying that "miracles still do happen, and miracles are caused by people."[57] And they are caused by God who is the author of all life and hope.

For those who would lose heart, watch the world around you, for it is true, miracles are happening. Watch and give thanks. Watch and give thanks whenever you see indications of healthy change in society. Last week it was the story of Balbir Mathur and his 900,000 trees. The week before it was announced that a company building a coal-fired power plant in a small eastern Connecticut town (Montville) is also planning to plant 52 million trees in Guatemala in order to offset the plant's contribution to the greenhouse effect.[58]

Working in the defense industries in California's Silicon Valley finally got to a small group of people who began to have questions about how they made their money and how their work was contributing to the proliferation of defense contracting in their area. They quit their jobs and began the Beyond War movement, a citizens' effort to alert the public about the dangers of the nuclear buildup.

No less than four of our nation's major defense industry plants (Rocky Flats, near Boulder, Colorado; Savannah River, at Aiken, South Carolina; Fernald, near Cincinnati, Ohio; and Hanford, in the state of Washington) have been shut down within the last four months, in every case because either plant neighbors or workers' protests to highlight safety hazards have finally been successful. A suit brought by some 14,000 southern Ohio residents led to the closing of the Fernald plant. It should also be noted that civilian nuclear facilities have not fared much better. Again, largely as a result of effective citizen action no public utility has planned a new nuclear power plant since the 1970s. Currently there are two completed nuclear power plants that will probably never be activated: the Shoreham plant on Long Island and Seabrook in New Hampshire. Similarly, toxic waste dumps are in trouble. The nation's first permanent repository for the nuclear waste from nuclear armaments facilities at Carlsbad, New Mexico, developed a water leak, just prior to its opening, that threatened to contaminate local water supplies.

That the nuclear industry's litany of disasters is now public is a first step in overcoming some of the dangers posed by our nuclear world. They are warnings. The alarm has been sounded. Recognition of the problem is a precondition for its correction. Let us watch public awareness grow and, as we do so, take heart from Sweden, which is committed to dismantling its twelve nuclear power plants by the year 2010.[59]

Let us thank God that consciousness-raising and continuous pressure finally result in action. Sometimes change occurs slowly, but a first step is always an understanding of the need.

It took some fifteen years between the first warning of atmospheric ozone depletion and the first international agreement to curtail ozone-depleting pollutants.

Our homes are now more energy-efficient, also our appliances and automobiles. The recycling of household trash—once a project of only the most dedicated environmentalists—is now increasingly becoming a municipal project in more and more communities. Recently the United States Navy agreed to drastically reduce the plastic products (bags, plates, cups, plastic cutlery, etc.) that it sends out on its ships and that they eventually dispose of at sea.[60]

A few countries are now seeking to control their populations, such as China, for example.

Wherever areas of the nation once dominated by defense industry contracts seek to diversity local industry, that is cause for thankfulness. Take Palmdale, California, for example, home of Rockwell International. The city, which has thrived as an assembly site for sophisticated aircraft, is broadening its base to include retailing, manufacturing, and service industries.[61] The Raytheon Corporation uses its military radio technology to make microwave ovens; McDonnell-Douglas has a subsidiary that sells computer services to health-care institutions.[62] This just names a few. Hopefully, the day will soon dawn when these companies are completely out of the defense business. But they have made a start and this is cause for giving thanks.

Whenever we see instances of generosity on the part of corporations, whenever they forego opportunities for profit in order to contribute to the common good, there is cause for thanksgiving. Like Merck and Company, the giant American pharmaceutical company that is providing, cost-free, a drug (ivermectin) the company developed for people in areas of Africa, Latin America, and the Middle East to treat river blindness. River blindness, caused by small parasitic worms spread by black flies, breeds in areas of fast-moving rivers and streams in hot climates and affects some 18 million persons worldwide, sending many to premature death. Merck is committed to giving away the drug until there is no longer any need for it, which will take at least ten years.[63] Sure, the cynic might say, Merck is a huge and profitable corporation that can well afford to reach out. True enough, but that's not the point. Rather, Merck has chosen to do what few other companies have done. Whenever any company or a nation or even an individual overcomes greed and profit for the sake of the common good, that is reason for rejoicing.

Let us thank God when cities and towns across the nation begin to take action for the environment. Los Angeles, plagued for a quarter of a century with smog thick enough to wilt crops and obstruct breathing, through tough sweeping legislation, seeks now to clean up its air by the year 2009. The city of Minneapolis has banned most plastics from grocery stores and fast food restaurants until the city can work out an acceptable way to recycle plastics. And the people of the tiny and poor town of Preston, Connecticut successfully opposed a referendum that would have authorized the construction of a huge 600-ton-per-day trash incinerator, capable of polluting the air for miles around. Certainly the actions of these municipalities are cause for great thanksgiving; others will follow suit.

Finally, let us thank God that at last issues of the environment are becoming a part—however small—of our national consciousness. In 1988, *Time,* the weekly news magazine, departed from its usual custom of naming a Person of the Year and named our endangered earth the Planet of the Year. By way of preparation, *Time* assembled a distinguished group of scientists, administrators, and political leaders from five continents to talk together about our common environmental problems and produce a realistic action program. And the *National Geographic* devoted the final issue in its centennial year to planet earth. Embedded in the recesses of its arresting gold hologram cover is the question, ``As we begin our second century, the *Geographic* asks: Can man save this fragile earth?'' Surely these are indications of a subtle change of consciousness underway. We *are* beginning to think more about the world around us, and we are beginning to put thought into action.

My sisters and brothers, watch around you for signs of renewal and reform. They are everywhere. As you identify them, give thanks, for wherever new life and health are emerging from decay and despair, there God is at work caring for and renewing Creation.

Recall the scene in Exodus 14 when Moses was leading the Israelites out of Egypt to the Promised Land. The people were groaning and complaining. ``Did you have to bring us out here in the desert to die? Didn't we tell you before we left that this would happen? We told you to leave us alone and let us go on being slaves in Egypt'' (Exod. 14:11–12). And Moses himself was becoming distressed, wondering if they could make it, worried that perhaps he and the Israelites had attempted more than they could attain. Yes, Moses was even beginning to lose heart.

But the Lord said to Moses, ``Tell the people to move forward. Lift up your walking stick and hold it over the sea. The water will divide and the Israelites will be able to walk through on dry ground" (Exod. 15b-16).

Helen Caldicott posed the question, "Can we evolve spiritually and emotionally in time to control the overwhelming evil that our advanced and rational intellect has created?"[64]

Let us answer resoundingly, "Yes, we can and we must!"

Tell the people to move forward. Tell the people to move forward. Tell the people to move forward and choose life that we and our descendents may live.

Notes

Epigraphs

1. Donald Williams, quoted in *The Home Planet*, ed. by Kevin W. Kelley (Reading, Mass.: Addison-Wesley Publishing and Moscow: Mir Publishers, 1988).
2. Ibid., p. 81.
3. Ibid., p. 140.
4. Ibid., p. 109.

Introduction

1. John Baker. "Making Christianity More Christian" (Selwyn Lectures, 1986), p. 7.
2. E.F. Schumacher, *Small Is Beautiful: Economics as if People Mattered,* Perennial Library (New York: Harper & Row, 1973), p. 82. Originally published in London by Blond and Briggs.
3. James Irwin, quoted in *The Home Planet,* ed. by Kevin W. Kelley (Reading, Mass.: Addison-Wesley Publishing and Moscow: Mir Publishers, 1988), p. 38.
4. Ibid., p. 71.

Chapter 1. Granny Dodge's World

1. Ernest Dodge, *Morning Was Starlight: My Maine Boyhood* (Chester, Conn.: Globe Pequot Press, 1980), p. 15.
2. Ibid., p. 15.
3. Ibid., p. 24.
4. Ibid., p. 99.
5. Barry Lopez, *Arctic Dreams* (New York: Bantam Books, 1987), p. 85.
6. Walking Buffalo, excerpted from an address given in London, England, date unknown, in *Touch the Earth: A Self-Portrait of Indian Existence,* compiled by T.C. McLuhan, Touchstone Book (New York: Simon and Schuster, 1971), p. 23.
7. René Dubos, *The Wooing of Earth* (London: Athlone Press, 1980), pp. 66–67.
8. Lopez, *Arctic Dreams,* p. 180.
9. Ibid., p. 266.
10. *Charles Darwin's Diary of the Voyage of H.M.S. Beagle,* ed. by Nora Barlow (New York: Macmillan, 1933), p. 339.
11. Ibid., p. 364.
12. Annie Dillard, *Teaching a Stone to Talk: Expeditions and Encounters* (New York: Harper & Row, 1982), pp. 112, 113, 123, 124.
13. Ibid., p. 128.
14. *Book of Common Prayer* (Episcopal), p. 324, adapted.

15. Charles Wesley, "Love Divine All Loves Excelling," hymn #657, in *The Hymnal 1982* [Episcopal] (New York: Church Hymnal Corporation, 1985).
16. Martin Buber, *Paths in Utopia* (London: Routledge and Kegan Paul, 1949). p. 128.
17. Jonathan Schell, *The Fate of the Earth* (New York: Alfred A. Knopf, 1982).

Chapter 2. The Rape of Creation

1. General Farrell, quoted in *Brighter Than a Thousand Suns,* by Robert Jungk (Harmondsworth, England: Penguin Books, 1960).
2. Arthur J. Laffin, "The Nuclear Challenge," in *Swords Into Plowshares,* ed. by Arthur J. Laffin and Anne Montgomery (San Francisco: Harper & Row, 1987), p. 5.
3. *General Dynamics 1986 Annual Report,* p. 16.
4. Stephen Kobassa and Arthur Laffin, sample letter to Navy Secretary James Webb, Congressman Samuel Gejdenson, and Connecticut Governor William O'Neill. No date.
5. Laffin, "The Nuclear Challenge," p. 5.
6. United States Congress, Defense Subcommittee on the House Appropriations Committee, *Statement on the Posture and Fiscal Year 1989 Budget of the U.S. Navy,* ed. by C.A.H. Trost (March 1, 1988), p. 16.
7. Carl Sagan, "The Nuclear Winter," in *Beyond War: Selected Resources,* (Palo Alto, Calif.: Beyond War, 1985) p. 3.
8. Ruth L. Sivard, *World Military and Social Expenditures 1987–88* (Washington, D.C.: World Priorities, 1987), p. 8.
9. World Commission on Environment and Development, *Our Common Future* (Oxford and New York: Oxford University Press, 1987), p. 297.
10. Committee for a Sane Nuclear Policy (SANE), "Do You Know What Your Tax Dollar Buys?" A one-page fact sheet, March 1983.
11. SANE, "What Can Your Money Buy?" A one-page fact sheet, March 1983.
12. Richard Halloran, "Stealth Sheds Secrets, But Its Cost Stays Hidden," *New York Times* December 14, 1988.
13. SANE "Do You Know What Your Tax Dollar Buys?"
14. United Press International report in the *New Haven Register*, November 4, 1987.
15. Laffin, "The Nuclear Challenge," p. 9.
16. Sagan, "The Nuclear Winter," p. 3.
17. Sivard, *World Military and Social Expenditures 1987–88,* p. 23.
18. Jon Bennett with Susan George, *The Hunger Machine: The Politics of Food* (Cambridge and Oxford: Polity Press and Basil Blackwell, 1987), p. 25.
19. Ibid.
20. John H. Cushman, Jr., "The Stinger Missile: Helping Change the Course of a War," *New York Times,* Sunday, January 17, 1988, p. E2.
21. Nigel Hawkes, et al., *Chernobyl: The End of the Nuclear Dream,* Vintage Books (New York: Random House, 1987), pp. 60–61.
22. Frank Barnaby, ed., *The Gaia Peace Atlas* (New York: Doubleday, 1988), p. 102.
23. Hawkes, *Chernobyl,* p. 59.
24. Ibid.
25. Barnaby, *The Gaia Peace Atlas,* p. 102.
26. Robert C. Kiste, *The Bikinians: A Study in Forced Migration* (Menlo Park, Calif.: Cummings Publishing, 1974), p. 28.
27. Leonard Mason, "The Bikinians: A Transplanted Population," in *Human Organization* (Spring 1951), p. 11.

28. Congress of Micronesia, "A Report on Rongelap and Utirik: Medical Aspects of the Incident of March 1, 1954," as reported in *Collision Course at Kwajalein: Marshall Islanders in the Shadow of the Bomb,* by Giff Johnson (Honolulu: Pacific Concerns Resource Center, 1984), p. 12.

29. La Bedbedin, as told to Gerald Knight, *Man This Reef* (Republic of the Marshall Islands: Micronitor Book, 1982), p. 153.

30. Barnaby, *The Gaia Peace Atlas,* p. 102.

31. Johnson, *Collision Course at Kwajalein,* p. 12.

32. Hawkes, *Chernobyl,* p. 54.

33. Ibid.

34. Hawkes, *Chernobyl,* p. 57.

35. William Kittridge, "In My Backyard: A Visit to the Proposed National Nuclear Waste Repository," *Harpers* (October 1988), pp. 59–60.

36. "Greenpeace: Waste Will Contain Toxics," *Marshall Islands Journal* 19 (December 23, 1988), pp. 15 and 23.

37. "Team of Engineers Begin Year Long Waste Disposal Studies," *Marshall Islands Journal* 19 (December 23, 1988), p. 15.

38. Bennett and George, *The Hunger Machine,* p. 27.

39. Dwight D. Eisenhower, from the Nuclear War Study Group, reported in *Peace: A Dream Unfolding,* ed. by Penny Kome and Patrick Crean, Sierra Club Books (Toronto: Somerville House Books, 1986), p. 111.

40. Andrea Woods, quoted in "Contaminants Seeping Into Ground Water Supplies," by Paul Guernsey, *New York Times,* January 17, 1988, Connecticut section, p. 1.

41. ABC Evening News, October 6, 1988.

42. Dick Russell, "The Fouling of the Atlantic," *New Haven Advocate,* November 3, 1987, p. 8.

43. Ibid.

44. Ibid.

45. Mark Jaffe, "Waste Dumping at Issue," *The Day,* (New London, Conn.), Sunday, November 22, 1988, p. A14.

46. Russell, "The Fouling of the Atlantic," p. 6.

47. "Emergency Instructions In Case of Nuclear Power Plant Accident," *Norwich Telephone Directory,* Southern New England Telephone, directory advertising pages, p. 3.

48. Robert A. Hamilton, "Haddam Neck Facility on Anti-Nuke Group's 25-Worst List," *The Day,* (New London, Conn.), April 26, 1988, p. A4.

49. Van-Alden Ferguson, "More Millstone Workers Say Safety Complaints Bring Harassment," *The Day,* (New London, Conn.), October 6, 1988, p. B2.

50. Philip Shabecoff, "Study Shows Significant Decline in Ozone Layer," *New York Times,* March 16, 1988, p. A25.

51. Philip Shabecoff, "Scientists Agree Global Warming Difficult to Stop," *New York Times,* News Service in *The Day,* (New London, Conn.), July 19, 1988, p. A7; also Philip Shabecoff, "Greenhouse Effect Tied to Record Heat," *New York Times,* News Service, in *The Day,* (New London, Conn.), July 24, 1988. p. A12.

52. Editorial, *New York Times,* October 9, 1988, p. E22.

53. Shabecoff, "Greenhouse Effect Tied to Record Heat, p. A12.

54. Matthew Wald, "Fighting the Greenhouse Effect," *New York Times,* April 28, 1988, business section no. 3, pp. 1 and 8.

55. Marc Reiser, *Cadillac Desert: The American West and Its Disappearing Water,* Penguin Books (New York: Viking Penguin, 1986), p. 454.

56. Ibid., p. 457.
57. "Show Me—A Citizen's Action Guide to Missile Silos of Missouri," (Madison, WI: Nukewatch, 1987) no page.
58. Ibid.
59. "Peace Garden?—A Citizen's Action Guide to the Missile Silos of North Dakota," (Madison, WI: Nukewatch, 1986), no page.
60. Jürgen Moltmann, *God in Creation: An Ecological Doctrine of Creation,* (Gifford Lectures, 1984–85), tr. by Margaret Kohl (London: SCM Press, 1985), pp. 23–24.
61. Octavio Paz, *The Labyrinth of Solitude,* tr. by Lysander Kemp (New York: Grove Press, 1985), p. 57. Original pub. date, 1961.
62. Rollo May, *Love and Will,* (New York: W.W. Norton, 1969).
63. Konrad Lorenz, *On Aggression,* (New York: Harcourt, Brace and World, 1966).
64. ABC Evening News, February 4, 1988.
65. Claude Lewis, "Terrible Toll Exacted by Teen Violence," *New Haven Register,* July 7, 1987.
66. Ibid.
67. Connecticut Commission on Children, *The Changing World of Connecticut's Children,* (Fall 1987), pp. 13 and 17.
68. Ibid., p. 17.
69. Marian Wright Edelman, Wheelock College commencement address, in *Wheelock Bulletin,* (August 1988), p. 20.
70. Ibid.
71. Lewis, "Terrible Toll Exacted by Teen Violence."
72. Ibid.
73. Paul Hodel, newsletter of the Peace Education and Action Center, no. 77 (February-March, 1988), p. 1.
74. World Bank, *Annual Report,* 1984.
75. Bennett and George, *The Hunger Machine,* p. 14.
76. Sivard, *World Military and Social Expenditures 1987–88,* map no. 3, p. 24.
77. Ibid.
78. Josue de Castro, *Of Men and Crabs,* quoted in Bennett and George, *The Hunger Machine,* p. 21.

Chapter 3. The Goodness of Creation: Biblical Motifs

1. Everett Fox, *In the Beginning: A New English Rendition of the Book of Genesis* (New York: Schocken Books, 1983), p. xxxvi.
2. Claus Westermann, *Creation,* tr. by John J. Scullion (London: SPCK, 1974), pp. 36–37.
3. Alan Richardson, *Genesis 1–11: The Creation Stories and the Modern World View,* (London: SCM Press, 1966), p. 29. Original pub. date, 1953.
4. Ibid., p. 30.
5. Westermann, *Creation,* p. 74.
6. Hayim Donin, compiler, *Sukkot,* part of a series, *Popular History of Jewish Civilization,* ed. by Raphael Posner (New York: Leon Amiel Publisher, 1974), p. 3.
7. St. Francis of Assisi, *The Writings of St. Francis of Assisi,* ed. by Benen Fahy (Chicago: Franciscan Herald Press, 1964), pp. 130–31.
8. Sidney Greenberg, compiler and tr., *Likrat Shabatt: Worship, Study and Song* (Bridgeport, Conn.: Prayer Book Press, 1977), p. 102.
9. Josef Pieper, *Leisure: The Basis of Culture,* Mentor Book (New York: New American Library, 1963), pp. 42, 43, 41.

10. Abraham E. Millgram, *Jewish Worship* (Philadelphia: Jewish Publications Society of America, 1971), p. 91.
11. Ibid., p. 92.
12. Matthew Fox, *Original Blessing* (Santa Fe, N. Mex.: Bear and Company, 1983), p. 48.
13. Richardson, *Genesis 1–11*, p. 72.
14. Walter Rauschenbusch, *A Theology for the Social Gospel* (Nashville: Abingdon Press, 1945), p. 33. Original pub. date, 1917.
15. *Catholic Social Teaching and the U.S. Economy,* first draft of the bishops' pastoral, in *Origins,* 14, (November 15, 1984), p. 345.
16. William James, *The Varities of Religious Experience* (New York: Mentor Books, 1958), pp. 137–38.
17. Zvi Adar, *Humanistic Values in the Bible* (New York: Reconstructionist Press, 1967), p. 137.
18. Kim Yong-Bock, "Biblical Relections on Covenant," Justice, Peace and the Integrity of Creation unit (JPIC), World Council of Churches, (Paper delivered at JPIC consultation, Glion, Switzerland, November 7, 1986), p. 8.
19. "Report of the Standing Commission on Peace," *The Blue Book: Reports of the Committees, Commissions, Boards and Agencies of the General Convention of the Episcopal Church,* (July, 1988), p. 352.
20. Vine Deloria, Jr., *God Is Red,* Delta paperback (New York: Dell Publishing, 1973), p. 98.
21. Catholic bishops' pastoral, *Catholic Social Teaching and the U.S. Economy,* p. 345.

Chapter 4. Turning from Creation

1. For a fuller treatment of the church at the beginning of the Reformation, please see Anne Rowthorn, *The Liberation of the Laity* (Wilton, Conn.: Morehouse-Barlow, 1986), chap. 4, "The Clerical Captivity of the Church," pp. 27–46.
2. Ibid., p. 39.
3. Jürgan Moltmann, *God in Creation: An Ecological Doctrine of Creation* (London: SCM Press, 1985), p. 36.
4. Jacques Ellul, *The Technological Society,* tr. by John Wilkinson, Vintage Books (New York: Random House, 1964), p. 329.
5. Claus Westermann, *Creation,* tr. by John J. Scullion (London: SPCK, 1974), p. 2.
6. Jeremy Rifkin, *Algeny* (Hammondsworth, Middlesex, England: Penguin Books, 1984), p. 108.
7. Karl Marx and Friedrich Engles, "The Manifesto of the Communist Party," in *The Marx-Engles Reader,* ed. by Robert C. Tucker, 2d ed., (New York: W.W. Norton, 1972), p. 489.
8. Friedrich Engles, "Socialism: Utopian and Scientific," in Tucker, ed., *The Marx-Engles Reader,* p. 697.
9. Moltmann, *God in Creation,* p. 28.
10. Frederick Lewis Allen, *The Big Change: America Transforms Itself 1900–1950,* Perennial Library (New York: Harper & Row, 1952), p. 4.
11. John A. Garrity and Peter Gay, *The Columbia History of the World* (New York: Harper & Row, 1981), p. 844.
12. Lewis Mumford, *The Myth of the Machine* (New York: Harcourt, Brace and World, 1967), pp. 272–75).
13. Westermann, *Creation,* p. 3.

14. Walter Rauschenbusch, *A Theology for the Social Gospel* (Nashville: Abingdon Press, 1945), p. 36. Original pub. date, 1917.

15. Tennessee Williams, *The Glass Menagerie,* New Classics (New York: New Directions Books, 1970), p. 1.

16. Isabel Leighton, *The Asperin Age: 1919–1941* (New York: Simon and Schuster, 1949), preface.

17. U.S. Department of Statistics, Bureau of Census, *Historical Statistics of the United States from Colonial Times to 1957* (Washington, D.C.: Government Printing Office, 1958), p. 135.

18. John Steinbeck, *The Grapes of Wrath* (New York: Viking Press, 1939), p. 117.

19. Huey Long, quoted in Arthur M. Schlesinger, Jr., *The Politics of Upheaval* (Boston: Houghton Mifflin, 1960), p. 20.

20. Arthur M. Schlesinger, Jr., "Broad Achievement of the New Deal," in *New Deal: Revolution or Evolution?* ed. by Edwin C. Rozwenc (Boston: D.C., Heath, 1949), p. 101.

21. Henry Steele Commager, "Twelve Years of Roosevelt," in Rozwenc, *New Deal,* p. 25.

22. Warren Susman, ed., *Culture and Commitment: 1929–1945* (New York: George Braziller, 1973), p. 8.

23. Richard Schickel, *The Disney Version: The Life, Times, Art and Commerce of Walt Disney* (New York: Simon and Schuster, 1968), pp. 141–42.

24. Ibid., p. 28.

25. Robert DeRoos, "The Magic Worlds of Walt Disney," *National Geographic* (August 1963), p. 161.

26. Schickel, *The Disney Version,* p. 154.

27. Ibid., p. 142.

28. Philip B. Kunhardt, Jr., ed., *The 100 Events That Shaped American Life* (*Life Magazine* special report, 1975), p. 27.

29. William H. Whyte, Jr., *The Organization Man,* Anchor Books (Garden City, N.Y.: Doubleday, 1957), p. 184.

30. Levittown brochure, quoted in *The Suburban Environment: Sweden and the United States,* by David Popenoe (Chicago: University of Chicago Press, 1977), p. 112.

31. Ira G. Zepp, Jr., *The New Religious Image of Urban America: The Shopping Mall as Ceremonial Center* (Westminster, Md.: Christian Classics, 1986), p. 150.

32. Walt Disney, quoted in "The Magic Worlds of Walt Disney," by DeRoos, p. 192.

33. Ibid.

34. Ibid., p. 182.

35. Ibid.

36. Joseph Judge, "Florida's Booming—and Beleaguered—Heartland," in *National Geographic* 144, (November 1973), p. 588.

37. Otto Rank, *Beyond Psychology* (New York: Dover Books, 1958), pp. 58–59. Original pub. date, 1941.

Chapter 5. Causes and Consequences

1. Philip Shabecoff, "Ozone Pollution Is at Peak In Summer Heat," *New York Times,* July 31, 1988, pp. 1 and 24.

2. Editorial, *The Day* (New London, Conn.), July 29, 1988, p. A10.

3. Associated Press, "Starvation looms in 'han baozi,' dried bun, of China," *The Day* (New London, Conn.), July 28, 1988, p. 72.

4. CBS Evening News, August 30, 1988.

5. John Teare and Stephen Stuebner, "Parachuting Firefighters Get Drop on Blazes," Gannet News Service, in *Detroit Free Press,* July 8, 1988, pp. 3A and 7A.

6. Keith Schneider, "Big Losses Ahead for Corn Crop," *New York Times* News Service, in *The Day* (New London, Conn.), July 13, 1988, pp. 1 and 12.

7. Justice, Peace and the Integrity of Creation (JPIC), "The Ecumenical Movement and Peace Positions: A Discussion Paper," resource no. 3, 4 (Geneva: World Council of Churches, 1988), p. 7.

8. Ibid.

9. Ibid.

10. Arthur Caplan, "The Hypocrisy of Americans About Health Care," *The Day* (New London, Conn.), March 8, 1989, p. A7.

11. Owen Chadwick, *Western Asceticm* (Philadelphia: Westminster Press, 1958), p. 14.

12. Ibid., p. 20.

13. Ibid., p. 23.

14. Hans Küng, *The Church,* Image Book (Garden City, N.Y.: Doubleday, 1976), p. 81.

15. Anne Rowthorn, *The Liberation of the Laity* (Wilton, Conn.: Morehouse-Barlow, 1986), p. 31.

16. Wolfhart Pannenberg, *Christian Spirituality* (Philadelphia: Westminster Press, 1983), p. 29.

17. "A Covenant Manifesto For the Nuclear Age," World Alliance of Reformed Churches, 1981.

18. Jeremy Rifkin, *Algeny* (Harmondsworth, Middlesex, England: Penguin Books, 1984), p. 50.

19. Octavio Paz, *The Labyrinth of Solitude*, tr. by Lysander Kemp (New York: Grove Press, 1985), p. 108.

20. Ernest Becker, *Escape From Evil* (New York: Free Press/Macmillan, 1975), p. 24.

21. Ibid.

22. A.M. Hocart, *Social Origins* (London: Watts, 1954), p. 35.

23. Iona Opie and Peter Opie, *The Classic Fairy Tales* (London: Oxford University Press, 1974), p. 17.

24. Rifkin, *Algeny,* p. 252.

25. Robert Jay Lifton, *The Broken Connection: On Death and Continuity of Life* (New York: Simon and Schuster, 1979), p. 385.

26. Viola W. Bernard, Perry Ottenberg, and Fritz Redl, "Dehumanization," in *Sanctions for Evil,* ed. by William E. Henry and Nevitt Sanford (San Francisco: Jossey-Bass, Publishers, 1971), p. 111.

27. Konrad Lorenz, *The Waning of Humaness*, tr. by Robert W. Kickert (Boston: Little, Brown, 1987).

28. G. Clarke Chapman, *Facing the Nuclear Heresy: A Call to Reformation* (Elgin, Ill.: Brethren Press, 1986), pp. 3–41.

29. Lifton, *The Broken Connection,* p. 369.

30. Bernard, Ottenberg, Redl, "Dehumanization," p. 102.

31. Carl G. Jung, "Approaching the Unconscious," in *Man and His Symbols* (New York: Dell Publishing, 1968), p. 72.

32. John L. McNeill, *A History of the Cure of Souls* (New York: Harper & Row, 1951), p. 149.

33. "Sin," *Oxford Dictionary of the Christian Church,* ed. by E. A. Livingstone, rev. (Oxford: Oxford University Press, 1983), p. 1279.

34. Ibid.
35. Walter Rauschenbusch, *A Theology For the Social Gospel* (Nashville: Abingdon Press, 1945), p. 31. Original pub. date, 1917.
36. Reinhold Niebuhr, "Christian Faith and the Common Life," in *Christian Faith and the Common Life,* ed. by J. H. Oldham (London: George Allen and Unwin, 1938), p. 72.
37. John C. Bennett, "The Causes of Social Evil," in *Christian Faith and the Common Life,* ed. by Oldham, p. 192.
38. Sigmund Freud, *Civilization and Its Discontents,* tr. and ed. by James Strachey (New York: W.W. Norton, 1961), p. 101.
39. Konrad Lorenz, *On Aggression,* tr. by Marjorie K. Wilson, Bantam Books (New York: Grosset and Dunlap, 1967).
40. Becker, *Escape From Evil,* p. 96.
41. Ibid.
42. Jim Wallis, *The Call to Conversion: Recovering the Gospel for These Times* (San Francisco: Harper & Row, 1982), p. 32.
43. Lesslie Newbigin, *The Other Side of 1984* (Geneva: World Council of Churches, 1983), p. 23.
44. John DeGrunchy, *Cry Justice! Prayers, Meditations and Readings from South Africa* (Maryknoll, N.Y.: Orbis Books, 1986), p. 43.
45. Küng, *The Church,* p. 615.
46. Erich Fromm, *Psychoanalysis and Religion* (New York: Bantam Books, 1950), p. 4.

Chapter 6. Listening to the Land: The Witness of Native Cultures

1. Peter J. Powell, "The Sacred Way," in *The Great Sioux Nation: Sitting in Judgement on America* ed. by Roxanne Dunbar Ortiz (Berkeley, Calif.: American Indian Treaty Council Information Center/Moon Books, 1977), p. 64.
2. Black Elk, *The Sacred Pipe,* recorded and ed. by Joseph E. Brown (Harmondsworth, Middlesex, England: Penguin Books, 1971), p. xx. Original pub. date, 1953.
3. Vine Deloria, Jr., *God Is Red,* Delta paperback (New York: Dell Publishing, 1973), pp. 300–01.
4. Ibid., p. 38.
5. Justice, Peace and the Integrity of Creation (JPIC), "The Ecumenical Movement and Peace Positions: A Discussion Paper," resource no. 3.4, (Geneva: World Council of Churches, 1988), p. 12.
6. Carl F. von Weizsacker, "On a World Convocation on Justice, Peace and the Integrity of Creation: 4 Theses, resource no. 1.3, (Geneva, JPIC, World Council of Churches, 1988), p. 2.
7. Preman Niles, "Answers to Questions," (Geneva: JPIC, World Council of Churches, no date [probably 1988]), pp. 6–7.
8. Carol Hampton, "Integrity of Creation Conference," *Ikhana* (Summer 1987), p. 3.
9. JPIC, "Integrity of Creation: An Ecumenical Discussion," resource no. 3.3, (Geneva: World Council of Churches, 1988), p. 8.
10. Dorothy D. Lee, *Religious Perspecties of College Teaching* (New Haven, Conn.: Edward Hazen Foundation, no date), p. 13.
11. Jim Swan, "Sacred Ground: Myth and Science Investigate the Powers of the Earth," *Utne Reader* (September-October 1987), p. 67.
12. Ibid., p. 68.
13. Barry Lopez, *Arctic Dreams* (New York: Bantam Books, 1987), p. 34.

14. Ibid., p. 368.
15. Lao Tzu/Tao Teh Ching, *The Way of the Ways: Tao* tr. by Herrymon Maurer (Princeton, N.J.: Fellowship in Prayer, 1982), no. 29, p. 57.
16. Stanley Rowe, in *Our Common Future: Report of the World Commission on Environment and Development* (New York: Oxford University Press, 1987), p. 293.
17. Ibid., p. 238.
18. Letter from Chief Seattle to President Polk, 1852, in *The Power of Myth,* by Joseph Campbell with Bill Moyers (New York: Doubleday, 1988), pp. 34–35.
19. Walking Buffalo, in *Tatanga Mani, Walking Buffalo of the Stonies,* by Grant MacEwan (Edmonton, Alberta: M.J. Hurtig, 1969), pp. 5 and 181.
20. Peter Powell, "The Sacred Way," p. 64.
21. Ibid., p. 64.
22. A. Irving Hallowell, "Ojibwa Ontology, Behavior and World View," in *Teachings From the American Earth,* ed. by Dennis Tedlock and Barbara Tedlock (New York: Liveright, 1975), p. 172.
23. Luther Standing Bear, *My People the Sioux* (Lincoln, Neb.: University of Nebraska Press, 1975), pp. 275–76. Original pub. date, 1928.
24. Ernest Becker, *Escape From Evil* (New York: Free Press/Macmillan, 1975), p. 28.
25. Lopez, *Arctic Dreams,* pp. 178–79.
26. Alice C. Fletcher, in *Touch the Earth,* compiled by T. C. McLuhan, Touchstone Book (New York: Simon and Schuster, 1971), p. 176.
27. Dorothy Lee, "Linguistic Reflection of Wintu Thought," in *Teaching from the American Earth,* p. 140.
28. Hallowell, "Ojibwa Ontology, Behavior and World View," p. 172.
29. Powell, "The Sacred Way," p. 64.
30. Ibid., p. 64.
31. James Madison, *Federalist Papers,* no. 45.
32. Roxanne Dunbar Ortiz, "Indian Political Economy," in *The Great Sioux Nation,* p. 68.
33. Powell, "The Sacred Way," p. 66.
34. Robert Bellah et al., *Habits of the Heart: Individualism and Commitment in American Life* (Berkeley, Calif.: University of California Press, 1985), pp. 270–71.
35. Owanah Anderson, *Jamestown Commitment: The Episcopal Church and the American Indian* (Cincinnati: Forward Movement Publications, 1988), p. 10.
36. "Integrity of Creation: An Ecumenical Discussion," resource no. 3.2 (Geneva: JPIC, World Council of Churches, 1988), pp. 9–10.
37. Hampton, "Integrity of Creation Conference," p. 3.
38. Deloria, *God Is Red,* p. 287.

Chapter 7. Toward an Ethic of Responsibility: Ten Commandments

1. Lester Brown, in "Pollution Ills Stir Support for Environmental Groups," *New York Times,* August 21, 1988, p. 30.
2. Ibid.
3. St. Basil the Great, "Selections from Homilies on Genesis 1:1–25," in *Epiphany* 8 (Fall 1987), p. 30.
4. *Book of Common Prayer,* pp. 302–03, paraphrase.

5. Arthur J. Laffin and Anne Montgomery, eds., *Swords Into Plowshares* (San Francisco: Harper & Row, 1987), pp. 223–232. Benjamin B. Ferencz and Ken Keys, Jr., *Planethood* (Coos Bay, OR: Vision Books, 1988).

6. Ruth Legar Sivard, *World Military and Social Expenditures,* available from World Priorities, Inc., Box 25140, Washington, D.C. 20007.

7. Anne Rowthorn, *The Liberation of the Laity* (Wilton, Conn.: Morehouse-Barlow, 1986), p. 90.

8. Berne Declaration Group, as reported by Jon Bennett, *The Hunger Machine* (Cambridge and Oxford: Polity Press and Basil Blackwell, 1987), p. 209.

9. Vincent Rossi, "Christian Ecology: A Theocentric Practice," in *Epiphany* 8 (Fall 1987), pp. 10–11.

10. Hans Kung, *The Church,* Image Book (Garden City, N.Y.: Doubleday, 1976), pp. 82–83.

11. John C. Bennett, "The Causes of Social Evil," in *Christian Faith and the Common Life,* ed. J.H. Oldham (London: George Allen and Unwin, 1938), p. 195.

12. Leonardo Boff, *Jesus Christ Liberator: A Critical Christology for Our Time,* tr. by Patrick Hughes (Maryknoll, N.Y.: Orbis Books, 1978), p. 64.

13. Elisabeth W. Burdick, letter to the editor, *The Day* (New London, Conn.) October 29, 1988, p. A10.

14. John Snow, *The Impossible Vocation* (Cambridge, Mass.: Cowley Publications, 1988). p. 10.

15. Ibid., p. 3.

16. George Gallup, Jr., "Unchurched America Ten Years Later," discussion of a poll presented in Detroit July 6, 1988.

17. Parker J. Palmer, "Going Public: A Working Paper for Christians on the Renewal of the Public Life Washington, D.C.: (Alban Institute, 1980), p. 11.

18. Dietrich Bonhoeffer, *The Cost of Discipleship* (New York: Macmillan, 1959), p. 167.

19. *The Nuclear Dilemma: A Christian Search for Understanding,* Report of the Committee of Inquiry on the Nuclear Issue, Commission on Peace, Episcopal Diocese of Washington, (May 1987), p. 118.

20. Thomas Merton, *Seasons of Celebration* (New York: Farrar, Straus and Giroux, 1965), p. 3.

21. A.M. Hocart, *Social Origins* (London: Watts, 1954), p. 87.

22. Ernest Becker, *Escape From Evil* (New York: Free Press, 1975), p. 6.

23. Robert J. Lifton, *The Broken Connection: On Death and the Continuity of Life* (New York: Simon and Schuster, 1979), p. 159.

24. Michael Novak, *The Joy of Sports* (New York: Basic Books, 1976), pp. 42, 91, 43.

25. Octavio Paz, *The Labyrinth of Solitude,* tr. by Lysander Kemp (New York: Grove Press, 1985), pp. 52–53. Original pub. date, 1961.

26. John A.T. Robinson, *Liturgy Coming to Life* (Philadelphia: Westminster Press, 1960), p. 31.

27. Allen Turner, quoted in "Hard Corps Blues," by Tom Augst, *The New Journal* 19 (January 30, 1987), p. 20.

28. Ibid., p. 22.

29. Ibid., p. 22.

30. Ibid.

31. Ibid., p. 23.

32. Ibid., p. 22.

33. Gordon J. Stenning, letter to Gene Robinson, June 17, 1988, p. 2.

34. David Bosch, "The Alternative Community," in *Cry Justice*, ed. by John deGrunchy (Maryknoll, N.Y.: Orbis Books, 1986), p. 178.
35. Kairos Theologians, *The Kairos Document: Challenge to the Church* (Bramfontein, South Africa, September, 1985), p. 23.
36. Jim Wallis, *The Call To Conversion: Recovering the Gospel for These Times* (San Francisco: Harper & Row, 1982), pp. 116–17.
37. Richard Steele, letter to friends, May 17, 1981, in *Cry Justice*, p. 200.
38. Robert J. Kinast, from *Origins* (February 4, 1988), reported in *Initiatives* (June 1988), p. 1.
39. "A Chicago Declaration of Christian Concern" (Chicago: December, 1977), p. 3.
40. Arthur J. Laffin, "The Nuclear Challenge," in *Swords Into Plowshares*, p. 19.
41. Tao Tzu/Tao Teh Ching, *The Way of the Ways: Tao*, ed. by Herrymon Maurer (Princeton, N.J.: Fellowship in Prayer, 1982), p. 74.
42. Charlotte Libor, "A Church Helps Pupils Dream of College," *New York Times*, October 23, 1988, p. CN29.
43. Wallis, *The Call to Conversion*, pp. xiii–xiv.
44. Alexander Stewart, "Lambeth Report," *The Living Church* (August 28, 1988), p. 8.
45. Philip Turner, "Sexual Ethics and the Attack on Traditional Morality" (Cincinnati, Ohio: Forward Movement Publications: Spring 1988), p. 22.
46. *Kairos Document*, p. 24.
47. Arthur Laffin, in Associated Press, "Good Friday Protest Results in 11 Arrests," *New Haven Register* (April 18, 1987).
48. Carl Mitchum, "The Love of Technology Is the Root of All Evils," *Epiphany* 8 (Fall, 1987) p. 27.
49. Jeremy Rifkin, *Algeny* (Harmondsworth, Middlesex, England: Penguin Books, 1984), p. 254.
50. Leonardo Boff, *Way of the Cross: Way of Justice* (Maryknoll, N.Y.: Orbis Books, 1980), p. 80.
51. *Kairos Document*, p. 14.
52. Anne Rowthorn, *The Liberation of the Laity*, p. 54.
53. *Kairos Document*, p. 14.
54. Ibid.
55. Balbir Mathur, in "Kansas Man Sows Seeds of Dream," by William Robbins, *New York Times*, October 17, 1988, p. A14.
56. Ibid.
57. Ibid.
58. John Ruddy, "Trees to Offset Effects of Montville Project," *The Day* (New London, Conn.), October 12, 1988, pp. 1 and 4.
59. Nigel Hawkes, et al., *Chernobyl: The End of the Nuclear Dream*, Vintage Book (New York: Random House, 1987), p. 115.
60. Associated Press, "Navy being asked to help reduce plastic pollution at sea," in *The Day* (New London, Conn.), June 29, 1988. p. A4.
61. Richard W. Stevenson, "How Contractors and Their Towns are Adjusting," *New York Times*, April 3, 1988, p. E5.
62. Robert A. Hamilton, "Arms and the State," *New York Times*, March 2, 1986, sec. 11, p. 25.
63. Arthur Caplan, "The Hypocracy of Americans About Health Care," *The Day* (New London, Conn.), March 8, 1989, p. A7.
64. Helen Caldicott, *Missile Envy: The Arms Race and Nuclear War* (Harmondsworth, Middlesex, England: Bantam Books, 1985), p. 367.

Index

74878